The Moral Maze

D0302534

The Moral Maze
A Way of Exploring Christian Ethics

DAVID COOK

First published 1983
Fifth impression 1990
SPCK
Holy Trinity Church
Marylebone Road
London NW1 4DU

Copyright © David Cook 1983

Cover illustration: The maze on the cover of this book
is from *Greg Bright's Maze Book* (Latimer New
Dimensions 1973), copyright©Greg Bright 1973,
and is used by permission.

British Library Cataloguing in Publication Data

Cook, David
  Christian ethics.
  1. Christian ethics
  I. Title
  241   BJ1251

  ISBN 0 281 04038 9

Reprinted in Great Britain by
WBC Print Ltd., Bridgend

For Simon and Kenneth

Contents

Acknowledgements   viii
Introduction   ix
1 The World in which we Live   1
2 The Values that Surround us   18
3 Christian Values   42
4 The Approaches to Decision-Making   64
5 Matters of Life and Death: (1) Abortion   86
6 Matters of Life and Death: (2) Euthanasia   133
Conclusion   173
Further Reading   174
Index   175

Acknowledgements

The following biblical versions have been used in this publication by permission of the copyright holders:

The New International Version (NIV), copyright © 1978 by New York International Bible Society, first published in Great Britain in 1978.

The Jerusalem Bible (JB), published and copyright © 1966, 1967 and 1968 by Darton, Longman & Todd Ltd and Doubleday & Company Inc.

The Revised Standard Version (RSV), copyrighted 1946 and 1952 by the Division of Christian Education of the National Council of the Churches of Christ in the USA.

Introduction

This is a book to help students, pastors, priests and all thinking Christians to make moral decisions. It is not David Cook's view on every moral area. Nor is it a purely academic textbook. Rather it is an attempt to show one way of reaching moral conclusions. We do not know what the new moral issues of the twenty-first century will be. We do not even understand all the different aspects of the problems that confront each individual today. Yet I believe that we can, and indeed must, develop a consistent, rational approach to moral issues, which is a truly Christian one. Inevitably, this means that the person looking for the answer to his or her problem in these pages will be frustrated. I do believe that there are answers to most of these problems, but I am firmly committed to helping people come to their own conclusions and to recognize the *basis* and the *consequences* of their decisions. This book will introduce the reader to *one* method of making moral decisions. It is not *the* method, but one to be tried, tested, adapted and applied. Most of the time our responses to moral issues are almost automatic. However, when a new problem or a new aspect to an old problem arises, we need to be able to frame or rethink our moral stances. My hope is that in reading and applying this approach, we may all seek to discern the mind of Christ in the midst of the moral dilemmas of today and tomorrow.

My thanks are due to Peter Baelz for his initial encouragement to undertake the project, to Joy Rummey and Juli Wills for their practical help, and to my long-suffering wife and family,

Kathleen, Simon and Kenneth. All the weaknesses and errors are my own. Any good things I owe to too many to name, but to whom I am truly grateful.

DAVID COOK
Oxford
July 1982

1
The World in which we Live

Before we can make moral decisions, it is vital to understand the context of our decision-making. This means looking at the world around us. What then are the features of our modern world which form the backdrop to our morality? What forces pressurize us when we try to make decisions?

'We live in a modern world.' We all understand that sentence, but what does it actually mean? What is this modern world? What does it look and feel like? How does it operate? Simply because we are part of the modern world does not necessarily mean that we understand either that world or our part in it. Os Guinness has expressed the point succinctly, when talking about modernity: 'We do not see it because we see with it'. If this is true, it will not be easy to understand our modern world and that will mean an effort on our part.

Problems of grasping the nature of the modern world are not unique to the West. Recent events in Iran, and the programmes we see from every continent reveal the struggle of ordinary people to come to terms with the pressures of modern living in their traditional and institutional contexts. Our modern way of living affects all that we do and are. This means that our moral decision-making is affected by the pressures of the world we inhabit. If we are to understand what we are doing when we make moral decisions, as well as to make those decisions properly, we must try to understand the context in which these decisions are made. We do not operate in a vacuum, least of all in facing moral problems. It is the way the world is and the way people are that often pose these very moral issues. The background to decision-making may have a very great effect on the decisions made. It may shape the form and the content of the decisions. It may make our morality what it is. Our task then is to grasp the nature of moral decisions and the context in which we make them. To do this properly we need to know as much as we can about our context of life. That means examining the world in which we live and the values that surround us. What, then, are the obvious features of our modern world and way of life?

1   Modern man's experiences

(1) ALIENATION
Alienation is a technical word for a very common experience. It is the experience of feeling lost and alone. It is to feel cut off from people, things and institutions. It is to feel like a stranger living in a strange foreign land, which somehow or other is still home. Newly bereaved widows often describe what this alienation is like. Suddenly they are confronted with tax forms, death certificates, insurance claims and all the jargon that goes with these things. The widow is alone and confronted by a world that she does not really understand, though she has lived in it for many years. There are different aspects to this feeling of distance and being at one remove from things. People who deal with abstract ideas and concepts, like academics, often themselves seem removed. We picture the forgetful professor or the philosopher contemplating his navel as both living in ivory towers. They seem isolated from the ordinary and real. The harsh realities of living seem to leave them untouched. Some sociologists call this *abstraction*. It is to be removed from reality. But this is not simply a disease that academics catch. It affects us all in one way or another.

We suffer in our modern world by being removed from the things that matter. In our work-settings, the decisions that affect us deeply are taken without our consent or involvement. We are simply cogs in the machine. We are the disposable people of life, who are moved and removed by the world of big business and finance at its whim. We are often treated as less than human. We are depersonalized. What is essentially human in us is ignored. The same feels true in politics. Local and national governments are manned by politicians who seem to live in a different world from ordinary folk, or by faceless and nameless civil servants and bureaucrats, who seem oblivious to the real situations of people. Major and minor decisions which radically affect how we live are taken by such people at a distance from us. We are simply told that taxes will go up, prices will go up, and wages will stay down. We are not consulted.

It is little wonder, then, that we feel depersonalized and alienated. We feel that we have little worth or importance. We are unable to make a difference where it really counts. We feel lost and bewildered by that complex, remote world of power and decision-making. It is no surprise then that we try to escape from these feelings in various ways.

(2) FUTURITY

One well-trodden escape route is into the future. This is not to suggest that Dr Who's Tardis is readily available to all, but we all have imaginations, which we can use or which can be stimulated in provocative ways. It is no accident that many successful films today are based in a future world of science fiction. *Superman*, *Star Wars*, *Alien*, *Close Encounters of the Third Kind*, and *2001* are the block-busting tip of the iceberg of escapist films. They transport us to a future world, where goodness triumphs over evil. It is a world (or worlds), where the individual can still beat the system and save the world, with a little help from his friends. He wins against all the odds even if it means defeating the enemy single-handed. It is a short step to see the same escapism in the tremendous interest in astrology, the occult and the paranormal. This interest is part of the same desire to have more say in and control of the here and now. We feel that, if we understand the future, we may have more power in the present.

This same fascination with the future is evident in two burning issues of the day. These are nuclear power and the ecological crisis. The anti-nuclear lobby paints vivid pictures of a world devastated by a nuclear holocaust or by some insidious leaking radiation. It is a world of scorched earth, flattened cities and living skeletons. That future scenario is so horrific, it is argued, that the present must be transformed. We must do without atomic power, to preserve our world and ourselves. The same kind of argument is presented by those concerned about ecology. They evoke a world where natural resources are exhausted and human resources bankrupt. They see a world of too many people chasing too few resources in too small a space. We must live more simply now, so that the world will simply live then.

It is noteworthy that many, who find the lurid apocalyptic style in the Book of Revelation hard to swallow, find no problem at all with these new apocalyptic styles. We do not find it difficult to imagine the end of the world. But that flight into the future is designed to help us cope better with present reality. All too easily, however, it may become an end in itself and be nothing more than an escape from our inability to change the here and now.

(3) INDIVIDUALISM AND EXISTENTIALISM

A second escape route from alienation and abstraction is into the world of the individual. This may be summarized best in the ideas of existentialism. It is a revolt against two things. It revolts against the idea that reason (or the power of the mind) is able to solve the world's problems. Existentialism denies that thinking alone will show us either what the world is like or how to solve the problems we face. Reason takes you nowhere. It is only concerned with definitions and with what we know already. It is limited in scope and in its ability to meet people's real needs.

There is another sense in which existentialism is a revolt. It revolts against a romantic view of the world and of people. It believes that to think romantically is to deceive oneself. The romantic has a false and unjustified optimism about people and the world. The existentialist wants to drag the romantic away from 'airy-fairy' optimism about the future to the 'nitty-gritty' of the present. Existentialists believe in facing up to reality. They look to the 'magic moments' of life which encapsulate central human experiences. These are the moments of birth, life and death. They are moments when we feel awe, dread and wonder. They are experiences in situations where we ask fundamental questions. Who are we? Why are we here? Where are we going?

The existentialist does not believe that there are answers to these questions. For him, the world is meaningless. Everything is absurd. Yet the existentialist does not give up nor retreat into silence. Instead he or she retreats into the world of the individual. That world is an inner world. It is a world of intention.

If I am walking down the main street with the principal of my college, I may feel a surge of desire to have his post for myself. I may see a bus approaching and at that moment the desire is so overwhelming that I might push him into the path of the bus. However, just then, the bus driver might have a slight heart attack and lose control of the bus. It mounts the pavement and knocks me down. I am fatally injured. What does the onlooker across the street see? He may imagine that the heroic David Cook had sacrificed his own life, in saving the life of his principal in the nick of time. That would be wrong. Appearances may be deceptive. My evil intentions were quite different. The existentialist believes that what really matters is what happens inside us. What goes on inside us may never be revealed to anyone else. That does not matter. Inner experience is the essence of the individual. This is what makes an individual an individual, rather than simply part of a crowd. It is the freedom to make one's own choices. What matters is the exercise of our will. It is in choosing that we make ourselves what we are. It is not so much *what* we choose, but *that* we choose. Making choices is the mark of the authentic individual. When we are faced with a meaningless world and awful absurdity, we ought not to flee into the future nor try to reduce the chaos to a false order by the logic-chopping of reason. The lone individual shakes his fist at absurdity by choosing whatever he wants. Authentic existence is the life of individual choice. In some strange contradictory way, that is the meaning and purpose of mankind.

If we look closely at our modern world, we see signs of alienation, futurity and individualism. These are all also attempts to confront and cope with its problems. We need now to ask what forces create these problems.

(4) PRIVATIZATION

Like so much sociological jargon, this sounds more difficult than it is. Privatization is a process by which there is a cleavage between the public and the private spheres of life. In this separation of the two, the private realm becomes the important one for people. It is the unique sphere of individual freedom and fulfilment. At its crudest, sociologists are telling us that we are all schizophrenic. We live in two distinct worlds. One is the macro-world of the public arena. It is the world of the 'Them'. It is the world of government, the state, big business, unions, bureaucracy and authority in general. It is an impersonal world with its own complex rules and jargon. It is a foreign world to most of us. We do not understand how things work in it. We do not comprehend the language used. There are too many long forms with small print written in apparent gibberish. We are helpless and impotent in this macro-world, for we do not belong there.

In sharp contrast, there is the micro-world of the private. It is small and beautiful. It is the world of the family, leisure and home. It covers the realm of personal fulfilment. It deals with the areas of life we choose because they matter to us and we enjoy them. It is a world of genuine, felt freedom and choice. We feel confident and competent in this world. We retreat here when the big bad world outside becomes too much for us. Our micro-worlds are the places where we go to heal our wounds, to restore the balance of life, and to re-establish our personal worth.

There are many problems and dangers inherent in this division, but this does not change the fact that there is a growing gap between areas of life where we feel like persons in a game and numbers in a slot machine and the areas of life where we feel safe, secure and have genuine significance. A key mark of the experience of significance is our freedom to choose.

(5) LIBERATION

We live in an age of liberation movements. National and racial groups are seeking liberation. Minority groups organize and protest to try to achieve greater freedom. We talk of women's lib., gay liberation, 'Solidarity' in Poland, and 'freedom-fighters' in Africa. All these groups are seeking *freedom from* conditions and governments which inhibit and remove fundamental rights from them. Such liberation groups are also looking for *freedom to* do their own thing on their own terms without outside interference or control.

There is a long history of liberation movements and the demand for rights, which is typified by the American War of Independence and the French Revolution. Since then the stress on freedom and human rights has become a part of our thinking and outlook. Hunger strikers in Northern Ireland, coloured communities in inner cities, workers in Poland are bound together by a stress on what each group regards as their basic human rights and the demand for freedom to live as they wish without control by others.

(6) SECULARIZATION

Secularization is the process by which religious thinking, practice and institutions lose their social significance. We live in such a secular world. It is in contrast to the world of the Middle Ages, where religion was at the heart of life and of people's thinking. The role of the Church and religion was central and important. This is no longer the case. We have gone through a transition from beliefs, activities and institutions presupposing traditional Christian beliefs to a society where beliefs, activities and institutions are based on atheistic grounds. Our thinking, doing and being are done largely without reference to God, the Church or religion. This does not mean that there was some golden age when everybody was religious. Rather, it points to the influence of Christianity in education, culture and the framing of laws. The assumptions built into the framework of our society were Judaeo-Christian. Now these assumptions are being questioned and changed. We are now secular people. This is not just true of the intellectual aspects of society, but also in ordinary work and life. The assumptions we all make and the things we take for granted in our speaking, thinking and general living have nothing to do with religion.

How has this shift happened? Historically there are a number of reasons for the process of secularization. *Urbanization* drove people from the country and villages to large towns, where they lost their roots and where the Church never penetrated. Increasing *industrialization* with its mechanization and technology removed the worker from his craft and transformed work into a means of earning a living. Often that means of employment is depersonalized and repetitive. At the same time, there has been a shift in the way in which we are educated. Many parents work and save to give their children the chance to go to college or university. The young student returns home highly critical of his parents, their generation, the ideas they share and the society in which he or she lives. Why is this? It begins in the nursery class, where we encourage a child-centred approach to learning. That approach necessarily involves the *questioning of authority*. This is the special quality of the British educational system, in contrast to many others in the world. It gives people a critical ability to assess things. However, to be critical in this way requires the questioning of authority. Nothing is taken for granted. Nothing is immune from criticism. This critical anti-authoritarian style has undermined the traditional seats of authority like the Church and Government.

Perhaps the major factor in the growth of the secular mind has been the success of science. Science can send men to the moon, cure killer diseases and allow us to see what is happening in Australia and Japan as it happens; it seems unlimited in its capacity to improve the quality of our lives. Technology, or applied science, has revolutionized the things that we eat, the clothes that we wear, the way in which we travel and the jobs that we do. It is little wonder that we are greatly impressed not only with science, but also with scientists. They are the experts of our times. They are the modern priests who have power over the mysteries of life and who enable us to cope with life. As the influence of science has grown and developed in nature, biology, history, psychology and society, the influence of religion has diminished. The God who once seemed to know the solution to all the problems we faced, has been made redundant by new generations of innovative scientists and technologists. When we look for answers to the great dilemmas of our age, it is to science we turn rather than religion.

(7) REDUCTIONISM
The scientific experts are specialists in particular fields. By the very nature of things, it is no longer possible to know everything, as is reputed of Aristotle. Rather, it seems that modern experts

know more and more about less and less. Specialization in science is increasingly narrow. It is no surprise that those who work in a narrow area of knowledge might well imagine that their area is the most important one. This is the kind of thinking which had led to reductionism. It is the attempt to reduce complex situations to simple elements. For example, we regard the activity of the mind as a complex matter. The scientific materialist believes that it is possible to show that all mental capacities like thought, memory, will and intention, can be reduced to physical processes in the brain. There is no such thing as mind. The working of the mind is purely a physical affair. A different account of the same thing may be given by the behaviourist. He suggests that there is no such thing as mental states. Rather, such supposed states can only be understood as actual or potential behaviour. What we do shows what we think or feel about things. There is no inner cinema inside the person where mental events are taking place and showing what will happen. We simply use sloppy language to talk about overt behaviour and are misled by such talk into imagining mental realities, where there are none. Mental states may be reduced to behaviour.

Our concern is not the truth or falsity of such views. What matters is that these views, falling broadly in the realm of physical and social science, reduce a complex phenomenon in the world to a simple explanation. This reduced explanation is both necessary and sufficient, they suggest. It tells you all you need to know. The effects of this kind of reductionism on morality will be explored below. For the moment, it is clear that the current emphasis on science has led to a parallel reductionism. This strives to 'get behind' appearances to some simple, uni-level explanation. It is part of the scientist's armoury. We may paraphrase Occam's razor, 'Never accept a complex explanation, a simple one will do'.

(8) PLURALISM OR PLURALIZATION

To live in the modern world is to be confronted with a vast variety of world-views. Each of us has the freedom to choose from a wide selection of alternative outlooks on life. There are a number of reasons why this is particularly the case today. The first is *mass communication*. To sit through the 'News at Ten' is to be transported from Westminster to Washington, Cyprus to Saigon. It is to see how people live and act in every part of the world. This is even more the case when we leaf through the *Radio Times* and see the programmes from abroad and read about other cultures. The world is not far away. It comes each evening into our living rooms by means of the 'box' in the corner. Thus a variety of outlooks and different patterns of life come into our homes and stand in contrast to our own way of life. Such experiences must raise difficult and fundamental questions for us. These questions are put to us in a very forceful way. This is not a matter of taking or leaving it. The media methods of presentation pose stringent demands on us to react. Children's programmes like 'Blue Peter' can raise over one million pounds for good causes. Television affects our lives and there is great debate over the influence of the portrayal of violence and sexual expression. The world of mass communication confronts the ordinary family with alternative life styles in the comfort of their own home. Whether it is the life style of the Ewings in *Dallas*, the Richardsons in *Crossroads*, the Vietnamese from John Pilger, or the Americans from Alistair Cooke, we are shown different ways of looking at the world.

Popular Travel has also aided this process by enabling us to go to different cultures. It may be the Costa del Sol or the coasts of Brittany, but despite the presence of fish and chip shops, we know and feel that we are in a different culture. The dress, the buildings, the traffic, the language, the food and the smell, all add up to the excitement and challenge of being abroad. It *is* a challenge, for we soon discover that people do not act as we do and live very differently. It is normally the small differences that catch us out. In Britain, we leave a tip on the plate at the end of a meal and hurry out of the restaurant. In Poland, the tip must be given directly to the waiter or waitress independent of paying the bill and with some show of ceremony. In a cinema or theatre in Britain, we squeeze past people with our backs firmly towards them. In Poland, such behaviour would be the height of bad manners. You excuse yourself along the line of seated people face to face. Behind such simple courtesies are different outlooks on and attitudes to life.

But we do not need to travel abroad to know this. In most cities in Britain, we find areas where Asian or West Indian families live contrasting lives to those of their white neighbours. This is not simply a question of colour. It involves morality, culture, social patterns, language, diet, expectations and all the things that go together to make a people's heritage and way of life. At the same time as we have been increasingly aware of the *presence of difference in our midst*, our own traditional patterns of life have been under stress. Economic forces and the explosion of knowledge and technology have made it necessary for most people to move away from home and family and find work in a new area. Such social, economic and geographical mobility has loosened traditional family life and accepted patterns of living. Not only are we free to choose different ways of living, but also we have to adapt ourselves to the new demands of modern living with all its pressures. Husbands and wives, children and parents, workers and management, teachers and pupils relate in a whole variety of different ways. There is no one simple pattern for each relationship that may be adopted. Circumstances force us to re-think how we live with each other. Why should it be like that, rather than like this?

The presence of others makes new possibilities for ourselves. Alternative life styles are readily available. The challenge of different ways of life is that it not only gives us an opportunity to be different, but also forces us to ask why we should continue to remain the same. The variety of world views has confused us and made us uncertain about the value and legitimacy of our own way of doing things. Why should we be totally right and everyone else wrong? What is so special about the way we do things? Perhaps there is something to be learned from other ways of looking at the world. For some, this leads to meditation and following a guru, for others it is a chance to begin their education again through the Open University. For some, it is Malta this year and Singapore the next.

(9) RELATIVISM

There is a philosophical position which matches the sociological process of pluralization. It is the philosophy of relativism. This denies that there are any absolutes at all. Things are only right and wrong, good or bad, in relation to a particular context. The relativist delights in the diversity of cultures and outlooks. He is usually a sociologist or anthropologist and sets himself the task of describing the different contexts in full. This in itself is not only innocuous but also very helpful. The danger in relativism comes when the relativist moves from the descriptive to the prescriptive. He ceases simply describing different ways of life, and begins to suggest that we should adopt a moral strategy in light of the differences. We are to tolerate differences and accept them. 'Live and let live', should be our motto. Tolerance is propounded as the main virtue. In the next chapter we shall see how this operates in a moral context and some of the problems such a view faces.

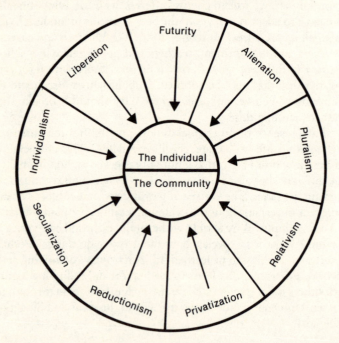

Our aim so far in this chapter has been to begin to understand the world in which we live. In order to do this, we have examined some main forces at work in our modern world. These forces have a radical effect on all that we do, but our interest is in their impact on religion and morality. Religion has been pushed from a comparatively central role in society to the fringes of human concern. The process of secularization has made religion seem redundant and provides explanations simply in terms of this world in the here and now. The effect of secularization has been to drive people into the realm of the private ghetto and into the power of the scientific experts. These are not value judgements so much as descriptions of how things have happened. Individuals have constructed their own worlds of meaning and purpose and created their own personal realm of safety, security and worth. At the same time, the explanatory power of science and its technological success has led both to optimism concerning the ability of science and scientists to solve the world's problems as well as to a reductionism on the part of some scientists. This reductionism seeks to reduce religion and morality to some simple, scientific level of explanation. The presence of alternative life-styles and world views has emphasized this search for explanation. The pluralistic world in which we live has encouraged the philosophy of relativism, which denies absolutes and upholds tolerance as the primary virtue.

2 The impact of the modern world on religion and morality*

In the face of alienation and an escape into the future, religion has seemed to have been weighed in the balances and found wanting. It seems to offer no answer to the problems of abstraction, de-personalization and alienation. Indeed some critics suggest that religion must bear much of the responsibility for such a sense of lostness and hopelessness. Traditionally, Christianity has pointed to the future as a ground of hope not only for individual survival, but also for transformation of the world and society. Sadly, this future hope has failed to change the realities of the present and been simply an unlikely escape from responsibility. At least the ecology lobby and the anti-nuclear protesters are grimly deter-

---

* In this section we will concentrate on religion, leaving morality to the next chapter.

---

mined to change the present situation. It is little wonder that both religion and morality have moved towards the stress on the individual and personal. If the issues of the world are complex, the retreat to individuality offers some hope of certainty. The Church has always been in danger of a retreat into pietistic individualism. The modern emphasis of existentialism provides an excellent vehicle for the implementation of that pietism.

Some theologians and moralists have jumped on the band-wagon of existentialism eagerly. They have used the existentialist analysis of mankind's situation and the nature of man as a means to summon people to authentic life. Such life begins with a moment of authentic decision-making. This is cast into a religious mould to follow the example of Jesus, who is portrayed as the authentic man. Morality has likewise followed the emphasis on individual choice as a means of security and as providing a solid foundation for moral choice. (See pp. 34ff)

The impact of privatization has reinforced the moves of religion and morality into the personal and private realm. Individual rights and freedoms have become the key moral notions, as may be seen in the various philosophers of liberation, while both religion and morality have moved away from the rational to the realm of feeling. We shall see how this operates in the moral realm presently, but it is clear that modern religious practice and emphasis is on personal experience, as the proper basis of religion. The music, the worship, the evangelism and apologetics (or rather the lack of them) all reveal a dependence on and a desire to cultivate particular experiences and feelings. There is little attempt at rational persuasion or debate. There is a flight from the mind into the realm of the subjective. The price of such a flight is high. It undermines notions of objective truth and it reinforces a fragile and limited world view, which is vulnerable to change and pressure from other sources.

In the face of the process of secularization the Church has re-treated. It has stressed inner experience at the cost of outer reality. It has emphasized one's own relationship to God as if that were independent of relationships with others. The Church has allowed God to be used as a plug for gaps in our knowledge. God became the god of the gaps. As the gaps decreased, so did the necessity for

God. Religion has emphasized the gap between the sacred and the secular. It retreated into the sacred realm and left the secular to the gods of this world. All too often this led the Church to emphasize ritual, mystery and the cultural forms and expressions of religion, rather than the realities to which these forms and expressions pointed. People are often more interested in the so-called dramatic spiritual gifts, like glossolalia and prophecy, than in the God who gives such gifts. The Church also allowed the secular world to force it into a mould, where religion was tied to outdated views of science and metaphysics, rather than free to pass judgement on all such philosophies. There is too much written on secular theology and secularized theology for us to add to that. Nevertheless, it is instructive to see how theology has been increasingly shaped and dominated by the challenges of secularism (the philosophy of the secular) and secularization (the process).

In the growth of industrialization, urbanization, the questioning of authority, and the development of science, religion and the Church have failed to make many notable contributions. They have been victims rather than victors and have seemed increasingly irrelevant to more and more people. Inevitably, reductionism has had a field day with religion and morality. Both have been reduced to psychological needs, social pressures, or economic necessities, and all too often there has been little critical response to such reductionist attacks.

The sense of the irrelevance of religion has been reinforced by the pressures from pluralization and relativism. Christianity has seemed to be simply one option among many. Its absolute claims have been doubted and its intolerance of alternatives a direct challenge to the easy-going acceptance of the relativist. The impact has not only been on how others regard the Christian religion. There has also been some direct effect. Once upon a time, there seemed to be a clear Christian line on most moral issues. Now it seems as if any moral view will be held by Christians. The recent debates concerning homosexuality and divorce and re-marriage illustrate the point. Some Christians are arguing that homosexual relationships are proper expressions of human love, while others stress that Scripture and tradition condemn such practices, and so must we. Some Christians believe it is not only wrong but actually impossible for anyone to be remarried in church. Once you are married you remain married, and a legal divorce does not alter that. Other Christians stress the ministry of compassion and forgiveness of the Church. There must be opportunity for a new start with God's help in a new marriage in church.

Such moral diversity among Christians is sadly matched by doctrinal diversity. Some Christians believe that the incarnation is simply a myth and was not an actual historical event. Others respond that this scepticism is unwarranted and that God became incarnate in the Very God, Very Man, Jesus, in the real processes of history. Thus in life styles and in even basic beliefs, Christianity seems to be as pluralistic as the rest of society. It also seems much influenced by relativism.

The main challenge of relativism has been felt in biblical studies. The biblical writings are historical documents. This means that they were written from a particular context to a particular setting. The relativist suggests that any truth the biblical documents have is truth only for that time and setting. This undermines the traditional pattern of the Christian use of the Bible. Christians have accepted a strong notion of biblical authority, recognizing Scripture as God's word for all mankind. Some biblical scholars have followed a relativist line and have been sceptical about the possibility of applying biblical teaching to our modern world. This same process has been reinforced by the tendency of some Christians to use the Bible in a subjective way. Their approach to Scripture is the 'Jack Horner' method of putting in a finger and pulling out plums. On this approach, the Bible means only what the Bible means to them. Truth is relative to their experience and thus entirely subjective. Religion is thus purely a personal preference. You can take it or leave it. Most of our contemporaries are perfectly happy to leave it.

Conclusion

We have followed some of the ways in which the modern world has had a serious impact on religion and morality. This gives us some understanding of the general context for decision-making.

We now move to consider the kind of moral values that surround us. In the next chapter we shall be seeking to marry the philosophical approaches to morals with the ways people use moral values in making decisions.

2
The Values that Surround us

To make a proper moral decision we need to understand the world in which we decide. In Chapter 1, we have looked at our modern world and tried to see some of the important forces at work. These forces radically affect our moral decisions for they shape the values we all hold. Christian and non-Christian alike cannot escape from the impact of the modern world. This chapter has been generally sociological in trying to describe our modern society in the forces and the ideas which shape the forms of life we share. Now it is necessary to describe our modern society in terms of its moral values.

Our first reaction is to question whether modern society has any moral values at all. Such a reaction is both to exaggerate the scepticism and negativity of modern life as well as to under-estimate the fundamental role of moral principles. We all operate with moral frameworks, even though they may be very different from each other and may function on the basis of what another moral framework calls immoral. Someone may believe that it is wrong to be selfish and to make moral decisions on purely selfish grounds. Another person may believe that all of us are selfish and that morality consists of always looking after number one. When such a person decides in a moral decision, he will consistently choose the selfish thing because that is the essence of his moral framework.

One other reason which might suggest that there is little morality around today is the very diversity of moral views. In fact, this helps to show that we cannot escape from moral points of view and that moral decision-making is a fundamental part of human life. Indeed many philosophers have argued that the ability to make moral decisions is the decisive difference between human beings and the animal or the purely physical world. The wide variety of moral decision-making in all its many forms, yet essentially still moral, helps substantiate their view.

If I am going somewhere new for the day, I may ask a friend, who has been there already, what I should see on my visit. He might respond in two sorts of ways. He might give me an Ordnance Survey map of the area. This would provide me with great detail and totally accurate information about the place, the amenities and its environment. This is fine, if I have time both to visit all the obscure and out-of-the-way places and to decipher the technical jargon of the map-makers. If I complain to my friend that I don't have the time or the expertise for the Ordnance Survey map, he might jot down a rough map of the area, highlighting the central and important places to visit. This well serves my purpose for a brief visit. In looking at the values that surround us, we are in need of a map. Like the visitor needing some help, we might have two levels of map to help us. The first would be a detailed technical picture of the exact situation in the moral area today. The other would be a general guide, which tried to highlight the important things and to give an overall feel of the values present in society. The first map-making task belongs to the technical moral philosopher and moral theologian. The second map is the one that we shall follow, because our aim is to see the general context and to highlight the important themes without every detail. This means that the perspective of the map is limited. Our map of morality is designed to give an overall impression which is accurate, yet is not nearly so carefully expressed or documented as the detailed maps of the moral cartographers.

Every map, even a simple one, is made up of different elements. Our map begins by making an assumption. It assumes that the general values in our society begin and end with human experience of this world. To put it another way, our map will present morality without reference to God. It will try to outline man's morality if he begins from the human alone. What, then, are the various aspects of human experience? Broadly speaking, we may discern three particular key experiences we all have. These are *thoughts*, *feelings* and *volitions*. We can think and use reason. We can present and follow an argument in our heads as well as on paper. We can reflect on what we have experienced and we can come to conclusions about what we have done and will do. We all have the experience of thinking. In contrast, we have senses—touch, taste, sight, hearing and smell—which provide us with different sensations. We have experience of the world about us through our senses. We also have feelings of emotion. We feel sad or happy, angry, disappointed and a whole host of other emotions. We are feeling beings. Of course, we can think about and reflect on these feelings and sensations, but thinking about the sensation of touch or of anger is not the same as feeling the anger or touching something. I may shake hands with someone very famous and have a whole range of feelings from touch to pride and awe. Later on, when I refuse to wash my hand for days and remember that I shook hands with that famous person, I am thinking about what I experienced, rather than having the experience itself. We have sensations and experiences, which are distinguishable from our reflection on these sensations and experiences. We have feelings.

Likewise we have volitions. In other words, we exercise our wills. We decide to do or not to do certain things. We intend to do things and sometimes we actually get round to them, but we may also have all too many intentions, which are never carried out. I may be lying in bed thinking about getting up, but just to think about it will not move me from the warmth and comfort of bed. I need to exercise my will. I make the decision to get up and usually do get up, later rather than sooner. But there are other decisions I take or intentions I formulate, which I never complete. I may intend to telephone home to say I will be late that evening, but forget or be too busy. I said to myself, 'I will telephone home'. I formed the intention. I meant to do it, but I did not. These acts of will and intention show us that we do have volitions and make decisions.

It is important to realize that in describing human life in these three categories, we are *not* saying that they are totally independent nor that they have nothing to do with each other.

Indeed they would not be human experiences unless they had a great deal to do with each other. They are usually integrated with each other, and our thinking, feeling and volition normally go hand in hand. What is being said is that modern morality—especially among moral philosophers—consists of a debate about the *source* of morality. Where does morality come from? If we answer that man himself is the source of morality, we are then asked, 'Well, which aspect of human life is the source of morality?' Modern moral philosophers give three different answers to this question. Some suggest that *reason* is the basic source of morality. Others argue for *experience*, particularly sensations or emotions. Others point to *will* as the basis and ground of morality. Remember that this way of expressing the map is rough and ready and seeks to give an accurate but overall impression rather than a detailed technical description. We may now move to the specific elements of our map of morality.

The map of morality

If I begin with *reason* as the source of morality, that part of the map would look like figure A (page 22).

If I begin with *experience*, that part of the map would look like figure B.

If I begin with *will*, that part of the map would look like figure C.

When we put the various parts of the map together, we end up with a sketch like figure D.

1   Reason as the basis for morality

Many people are impressed by man's ability to reason and to think. From Plato (*c.* 430–347 BC) onwards some philosophers have tried to base their theories on this ability. When applied to morality, it comes to the view that by thinking alone you can arrive at moral conclusions. This has led off in two directions.

(1) NATURALISM
Some people believe that by thinking about nature it is possible to

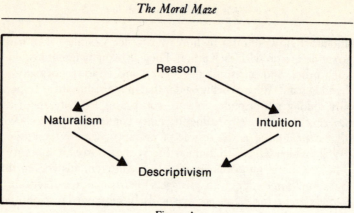

Figure A.

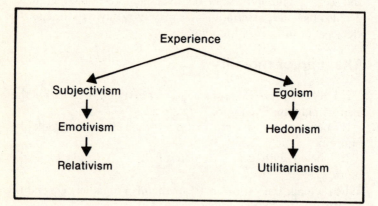

Figure B.

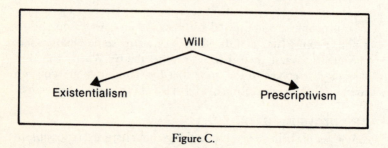

Figure C.

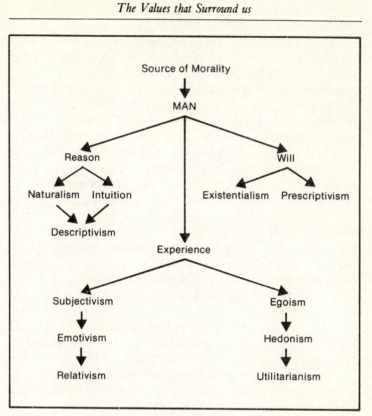

Figure D.

discern certain moral truths. By nature is meant two specific things. By looking at the nature of the world, you can discern moral truth. By looking at the nature of men and women, you can see moral truth. This basis of morality argues that there is in the nature of things or in the nature of people (or both together) a morality, which reason can discern. Goodness and badness are *natural* features of the world, of mankind or of both. This means that by looking at the way the world is, we can see a morality in the nature of things. If you do certain things, other things necessarily follow. The world is such that whatever is sown is reaped. The law of causes leading to effects holds in a moral sense as well as a physical. Likewise the nature of man reveals moral features. We come to understand that there are certain things, which are good for people, and other things, which are bad. Goodness and badness refer to the things which are good for people or bad for people. The task of the moralist is to think about the nature of the world and of people so that we may all come to understand what is good and bad. Thus it is possible for us to describe good and evil, right and wrong from the realm of nature and from human nature. These descriptions stem from the use of reason. By thinking about the world and human nature, we can come to moral conclusions.

(2) INTUITION

The heart of this view is that right and wrong are obvious to any and every reasonable person. If you put a person in a situation where they have to make a moral decision, the person will *know* what is right and wrong. By weighing up the situation, he will be able to come to understand what he ought to do or ought not to do. The use of reason will give him an intuition of right and wrong. Intuition is a direct kind of knowing. It is rather like seeing the point. When someone tells a joke, there may be a pause before the penny finally drops and the audience gets the joke. The moment of the 'seeing' of the joke is the moment of intuition. Parallel to this, the supporters of reason suggest, it is possible to intuit the moral point in a situation. You just know what is right and wrong, good or evil. You cannot explain it any further. Indeed, you do not feel that it needs any explanation. In other words, morality is self-evident.

The supporters of the view that reason is the basis for morality do not imagine that this self-evidence means that no work or effort is required in moral decision-making. On the contrary, by 'self-evident' they mean that, after, and only after, a process of deliberate weighing up of the situation, assessment of the facts and consideration of the consequences, it will be clear to any reasonable person what ought to be done. Of course, if you are unreasonable or irrational, you will not grasp the intuition.

The most obvious example of this kind of approach is conscience. When we are in moral dilemmas, faced with the necessity of making a moral choice, our consciences will tell us what to do. Conscience is understood as an inner voice which speaks words of moral guidance or of warning. People know what is right and wrong because their consciences tell them. They may still do what is wrong, but they *know* that it is wrong and what they are doing. This makes sense and because people are essentially the same—they have the same nature—our consciences will tell us the same sorts of things. The critic of this view will point to occasions when people's consciences tell them to do contradictory things. The believer in reason will then stress that in such a situation of conflict, the only way to resolve the point at issue is to offer *reasons* for your way of looking at things. That we justify, or try to justify, our moral decisions and conclusions proves that reason is really at the heart of morality.

(3) DESCRIPTIVISM

The two threads of naturalism and moral intuition come together in modern moral philosophy under the general title of 'descriptivism'. The descriptivist believes that there are moral facts in the world in a similar way to the existence of physical facts. We can understand morality by discovering and describing these moral facts. In teaching people to be moral or in justifying the moral decisions we reach, the descriptivist looks to reason to help us locate moral 'brute facts' and to grasp the significance of these facts. They are 'brute facts' because they are absolutely basic, and you cannot go behind the facts to another level of explanation. Explanations stop at these facts. There is nothing more to be explained and no other explanation is possible.

(4) SOME CRITICAL REFLECTIONS

Our real task is to see that there are in our modern world people who understand morality as having its source in reason. They appeal to the nature of the world, the nature of mankind, to intuition or to conscience as the material reason uses in making moral decisions. There are many lines of criticism against such views, and we shall simply mention some key problems to show that we cannot simply accept what moral philosophers may say, without thinking very carefully about it.

Does this kind of rational approach assume that people are totally reasonable? In fact, are not people all too human and influenced by a whole series of unreasonable fears, feelings and attitudes? Even if this were not the case, the rationalist approach seems more applicable to the highly intelligent than to the simple, down-to-earth ordinary person in the street. The stress on reason certainly seems to believe that people are reasonable and will be honest and act on the basis of their rational thought. Is this too optimistic?

Naturalism runs into other sorts of problems. What is natural to twentieth-century man is very different from what was considered natural to second-century people. Is there really any content to the notion of 'what is natural'? The intuitionist has similar kinds of problems. If it is possible to have an intuition, is it also possible *not* to have one? What do we do, if reasonable people think very hard about exactly the same facts in the same situation and yet come to different conclusions? Perhaps the key criticism against reason as the sole basis of morality is that, even when we *know* what is right and wrong, simply knowing does not help us to do, or not to do, right and wrong. Ethics is about doing; not just about thinking.

Of course, there are answers to these questions and the debate still rages on. To describe any more of the debate is to move into the ordnance survey area of moral maps. Our aim is to show how some people argue that the basis of morality is to be found by reason in nature or in intuition. They believe that it is possible to describe moral facts about humanity and the world. However, there are those who reject these ideas. They do not believe in 'moral facts'. They do not think that we can describe morality by reason alone. They turn our attention to feelings and experience.

2 Feeling as a basis for morality

When feeling is taken as the essence of morality there are two clear lines of thought. The first is that morality is about feelings in general. The second is that morality is about feelings of pleasure. We shall look at each line of thought in turn.

(1) SUBJECTIVISM

In modern times the great debate in philosophy has been between reason and experience. The *rationalists* argued that reason was the source of all knowledge. The *empiricists* argued that genuinely helpful knowledge came from sense experience. They did not say that reason gave no knowledge. Rather, they claimed that reason gave you no *helpful* knowledge. Reason only provided definitions and expressed what you knew already. In contrast, empirical knowledge revealed things that were genuinely novel and helpful. This view had many implications, but our concern is with the impact of such a rejection of reason on morality. If morality is not founded on reason, what is its basis? The subjectivist says that morality is purely a matter of personal taste and preference. What is good and right or bad and evil depend on me and my own feeling. People just happen to feel strongly about things. This is not reasonable. It is simply what they feel. This explains why there is such a wide variety of moral views. Different people have different feelings and so come to different moral outlooks. Morality is essentially a matter of personal preference. It is a question of taste.

(2) EMOTIVISM

The problem with subjectivism is that it does not seem to explain what we are doing when we make moral judgements. People do pass moral judgements on people and situations. What are they doing when they pass such judgements. The emotivist is a more careful proponent of the subjectivist line. He takes a situation where a radical feminist and a member of the Society for the Protection of the Unborn Child (SPUC) are in debate over abortion. The feminist says, 'Abortion is every woman's right. There is nothing wrong with abortion'. The member of SPUC argues, 'Abortion is wrong and evil. It is murder of innocent life. The foetus has rights, for the foetus is human'. The emotivist suggests that the debate may be characterized quite simply as follows:

> Feminist: Abortion—Hurray!
> SPUC member: Abortion—Boo!

Morality for the emotivist is to do with feelings. When we pass a moral judgement, he believes that we are doing two distinct things: (i) we are *expressing our emotions* on a subject. We are giving vent to our feelings. We are telling people that we feel and what we feel; (ii) we are *trying to encourage* others to feel the *same things* as we do. If I use the words 'right' or 'wrong', I am saying that I like something and I dislike something else. I am also hoping that you will like and dislike the same things. When we see posters of starving children on advertising billboards, the advertiser is trying to win over our feelings. We should end up by feeling sorry for the children and feeling guilty about our lack of concern. We should end up saying, 'It is wrong that people should starve'. The emotivist believes that we make such moral judgements on the basis of feelings. Feelings lead to actions. For the emotivist morality is a matter of the expression of feeling and the encouragement to others to feel the same.

(3)   RELATIVISM

The subjectivist and emotivist approach, which stresses the role of feelings, can end up in what is called relativism. If morality is purely based on feelings and emotions, then we would expect morality to fluctuate according to the person who has the feelings and emotions. In other words, this way of approaching morality ends up with the notion that morality is relative to a particular person (or group of people) at a particular place and time and in a particular setting. The relativist denies that there are any absolutes. Everything is relative. All moral rules, principles and outlooks depend on particular cultures and settings and the people in those settings. In Timbuctu, it may be 'right' to eat your grandparents while they are fit and well, in order to send them to the next life fit and healthy. In Taunton, it may be 'right' to put them in an old folks' home. In Tiree, it may be 'right' to take aged grandparents into the home, regardless of the effects of such action. People in each of these places would call 'wrong' what happens to grandparents in the other two places.

The relativist uses this kind of argument to show that what is considered 'right' and 'wrong' varies all over the world and indeed throughout history. Morality varies from time to time, place to place, society to society, and culture to culture. The morality of the Middle Ages is different from that of the twentieth century. The moral principles and practice in a hippy commune would differ from those in a Trappist monastery. But, so what? The relativist does not stop at stressing the relativity of morals, he then follows through with a particular recommendation.

In light of moral relativity, let us be tolerant. If morality is purely subjective and relative, then let us be less critical of others and less dogmatic concerning our own views of morality. Let us accept moral differences. Let us allow other people to do their own thing. Let us refuse to force our views of right and wrong on anyone else. Let us be tolerant. After all, 'right', 'wrong', 'good' and 'bad' are simply feelings. One person's feelings are just as valid as anyone else's. Let everyone do their own thing for moral integrity is about being true to one's feelings and convictions.

If we start with experience as the basis of moral judgement, we end up with an individualistic morality. Relativism means each person pleasing himself. It means doing your own thing and letting others do their thing too. There are no moral absolutes or fixed moral principles. Moral views are *not* true or false. They are simply matters of taste.

(4) SOME CRITICAL COMMENTS

Many people have doubted whether morality is really such a *subjective* affair. They suggest that there are *objective* elements to morality. They point to the general agreement in various moral codes to the centrality of murder and the sanctity of life, truth-telling and promise-keeping and some form of sexual ordering. It looks as if all moral codes have some moral expression concerning these themes, even though the details may vary. These common themes are, it is claimed, objective. A more substantial point is that, to talk sensibly about a moral issue at all, we must have some kind of agreement about what constitutes morality and what is morally relevant and irrelevant. If this was not the case, we could not understand each other's views. This is to say that moral argument, justification and debate presuppose an objective area to which we may refer and by which moral disagreements may be expressed and, in time, resolved.

The attempted reduction of morality to the realm of feeling alone has run into a number of problems. Even if it is true, as it undoubtedly is, that our feelings are involved in our moral views, it does not mean that our views are *based solely* on feelings. We can and do give *reasons* why we think things are right and wrong. The critique continues by giving examples of making moral decisions which run contrary to our feelings and desires. I may feel a great sympathy and concern for a naughty child, but I may still judge and punish his action as wrongdoing. I do my duty in spite of my feelings. To do what is right is *not* the same as doing what I feel like.

The relativist approach likewise runs into problems. The very statement of relativism seems oddly self-defeating. If there are no absolutes, can the relativist claim that 'everything is relative'? If this is an absolute judgement, it shows that there is one thing which is *not* relative, that is, the statement that 'everything is relative'. If, on the other hand, this judgement is, in fact, relative, it means that it is only relatively true that 'everything is relative' and that truth is only true in a particular context, at a particular time for a particular set of people. This kind of criticism tries to stop relativism before it even gets started. It suggests that relativism is literally nonsense. Others try to criticize relativism by examining its examples. Is there nothing in common between the behaviour of people in Timbuctu, Taunton and Tiree? It may be argued that they are all really showing the same kind of concern. They are concerned for the welfare of their grandparents and to do their best for them. They happen to have different beliefs about how to achieve the best, but they have a common, objective moral concern for older relatives.

The final line of criticism that we shall mention concerns the notion of tolerance. It questions whether tolerance is a proper conclusion to the problem of relativism. If relativism is true, tolerance is only relative to a particular context. It cannot have an absolute and universal application. Besides which, tolerance is necessarily limited when it is confronted with intolerance. To put it at its most pointed, we might ask, 'How tolerant can we be of the person who is intolerant of tolerant people?' May we tolerate ourselves out of existence?

None of the above arguments are meant to be a total answer to the view that morality is based on feelings in general. Rather they are designed to show some of the questions we ought to put to the proponents of the view. There is, however, another version of the 'experience-view' which suggests that morality stems from a particular set of feelings.

3 An alternative 'experience-view'

(1) EGOISM

The particular set of feelings which are often taken as a foundation for morality are those of pleasure. Behind such a view rests a general philosophy which we call selfishness and the philosopher calls egoism. Egoism is the moral theory that self-interest or selfishness is at the base of our moral views and attitudes. When we make moral judgements, we do so on the basis of pleasing ourselves. This general notion soon takes a very specific form called hedonism.

(2) HEDONISM

The hedonist believes that pleasing ourselves—or making moral judgements—is essentially the pursuit of pleasure and the avoidance of pain. We are all concerned to get as much pleasure as we can and to avoid as much discomfort and dis-ease as possible. When we make moral decisions, the hedonist suggests that we are judging what will lead to more pleasure either in a positive direct way, or an indirect way by avoiding pain. For some hedonists this description is purely psychological. It is simply a statement of how we actually function. People just happen to be motivated by pleasure. They try to do things that please them. They avoid doing things that cause them pain and distress. Others go a stage further and suggest that hedonism is a proper ethical view. It attempts to legislate what people ought to be doing in life. They ought to seek pleasure. The ethical hedonist is prescribing how we ought to run our individual lives and that of our society. This leads very naturally into the theory of utilitarianism.

(3) UTILITARIANISM

The chief proponents of utilitarianism were Jeremy Bentham and John Stuart Mill. Their own personal, political careers reinforce the aim of their philosophy. Utilitarianism is concerned with social reform. It begins by asking what kinds of laws we should have in our society. Their answer is laws which make people happy. This idea is still at the heart of government today. In the year 1981, Britain's government adopted a series of strict policies and harsh economic measures. Only the very foolish would imagine that these policies stemmed from sadism on the part of the government and a delight in the unpopularity which often accompanies the application of the policies. In fact, these harsh policies were seen by the government as essential so that *in the end*, the British people would be in a happier situation. We may be uneasy about the optimism, but the intention is clear. Re-election would be major priority and that would entail ensuring that the electorate was happier overall with the government's policies, than with those of another party. Our parliamentary and legal systems depend on this notion of making people happy or creating the conditions in which people may be happier.

The heart of utilitarianism is the Greatest Happiness Principle (GHP). It stresses that morality is about the greatest happiness of the greatest number. We ought to seek to create pleasure and to avoid pain for as many people as possible. Naturally, Bentham realized that for such a view to work, it must be possible to measure pleasure. He offered the following as a pleasure calculus:

Duration	—	How long it lasts
Intensity	—	How intense it is
Propinquity	—	How near it is
Extent	—	How widely it covers
Certainty	—	How sure we are that it will come
Purity	—	How free from pain it is
Fecundity	—	How much it will lead to more pleasure

Bentham believed that it was possible to give a specific content to the notions of good, bad, right and wrong, by reference to the amount of pleasure and pain in particular situations.

Mill tried to reformulate the utilitarian theory, so that it would avoid the problems of being unjust. As a lecturer, nothing gives me greater pleasure than the sound of my own voice in the presence of a captive audience of students. As a deeply sensitive person, my capacity for pleasure (and pain) is very great, so that when I consider how long to lecture to a group of students in a morning, I calculate a greater amount of pleasure if I perform for three hours than any shorter period. I might then calculate how much pain this would cause to the student body. One or two might become bored. A few might become stiff, but, in the end, students being fairly insensitive, the amount of pain involved would be much less than the total amount of pleasure I would gain. On a strict utilitarian calculation, I should then proceed to lecture to these mythical students for three hours. The problem is that our (and their) natural reaction is that this is unfair. There are more of them than me, so why should my pleasure be given preference? I might reply that on the grounds of *quality* and *quantity* my pleasure is greater. Still there would be the very strong feeling of injustice. Mill tried to counter this kind of problem by introducing a Principle of Justice (or Equality). It stated that everyone counted for one and for no more than one. Thus when we apply the pleasure calculus, we are also to be fair. Utilitarianism is thus concerned about the greatest happiness of the greatest number on a just basis.

We have seen that a philosophy of selfishness finds expression in the hedonist morality which sees moral decisions being made on the basis of pleasure and the avoidance of pain. This becomes a social theory in utilitarianism which is concerned to make moral judgements on the basis of the greatest happiness of the greatest number.

(4) SOME CRITICAL COMMENTS

Obviously there is considerable unease about seeking to base a morality on selfishness or on pleasure-seeking. What is this pleasure and how is it to be defined? Is it the same for all? What about sadists and masochists? In fact, morality seems much more about duty, obligation and responsibility than about pleasure. To do one's duty is not always pleasant, but it may still be right. I may be having a wonderful time doing something and derive a great deal of pleasure from that activity, but it is still proper, and necessary, to ask whether I *ought* to be doing this. The ought question is the moral question, and this is far more than pleasure.

Utilitarianism likewise runs into problems. It has been criticized as being only interested in the consequence of actions. Morality is *also* about *motive* and *intention*. Why we do something matters, as much as the consequences of our action. Indeed we may have little control over consequences, so it does not make sense to make us responsible for all the consequences. Bentham's calculus has also come under fire. Can we really measure pleasure or pain? What are the basic units of pleasure? Does the calculus really help and really work? How may I add my pleasure at a Scottish victory at Wembley, the enjoyment of a T-bone steak, and the money the Football Association gained from the football game? Some have argued that *quality* and *quantity* of pleasure conflict. Others have shown the tension between the Greatest Happiness Principle and the Principle of Justice. We might end up doing what the Chinese want because there are more of them.

4 The will as the source of morality

(1) EXISTENTIALISM
The last feature of our map of morality is the will as the source of morality. Here the temptation to give a detailed account is very great, but we have already seen something of the first form that such a kind of view takes. It follows the existentialist account of the world that everything is meaningless. Naturally, we might assume that this belief would lead to giving up all together. In fact, the existentialist urges no such thing. In the face of the meaninglessness and pointlessness of everything, the existentialist challenge is to create meaning by the exercise of the will. Morality is about my decisions. I create my own morality because I will it. I choose my own moral views. The way the existentialist proceeds is by examining impossible moral dilemmas. He chooses examples where no matter what we do, something will be wrong. If five people are trapped in a submarine with only sufficient air for three,

should the captain sacrifice himself and one crew member so that the others may live? Amazingly, none of the rest of the crew can navigate the submarine, so can the captain take his own life? The existentialist does not seek to destroy choice, but rather stresses that there is nothing else to do but choose. To be human is to make choices. Indeed our choices make us the people we are. Choice is thus central to life and to morality. We choose and create our own morality. To refuse to choose is itself to choose. To go along with the crowd, the past, or tradition, are all choices, but the only truly authentic choice is one in which we commit ourselves and the whole of our lives to the choice made. Inauthentic choices do not really count, for we refuse to live them out. Such a view of morality has been more popular on the Continent than in Britain. Perhaps it seems a trifle extreme for the phlegmatic Briton. In its place, however, Oxford scholarship has produced a more reasonable adaptation in prescriptivism.

(2) PRESCRIPTIVISM

Essentially stemming from Kant, it is still the case that prescriptivism has been much influenced by existentialist writing and the force of the moral dilemmas raised by that philosophy. The prescriptivist agrees with the necessity to stress the role of the will as fundamental to morality. However, the prescriptivist cannot accept the other things held by existentialists. The prescriptivist argues that, if we all choose individually, there would be no reason for our choices and no common life at all. To help correct this fault, the prescriptivist presents a reasonable existentialism. He does believe that the crucial part of moral decision-making is the will. However, he adds to that the *Principle of Universalizability*. It says that, when I choose to do something in a moral situation, I must choose what everyone else in the same situation would choose. It is as if, when I choose, it is really everyone choosing. This stops selfishness, pleasing myself and begging the moral question in my own favour. I have to choose for and in the same way as everyone else.

In this way, morality is seen as *prescribing*. In making a moral judgement I am prescribing not only what I should do, but also what everyone else should do when faced with the same situation.

(3) SOME CRITICAL COMMENTS

The critics of existentialism suggest that the philosophy as a whole is at fault. If this is so, then its doctrine of choice will run into problems too. The attack on the over-emphasis on choice centres on the failure to put choice in the context of reason and feeling. Even to frame the terms of a choice requires something more than the act of will. Besides which, it is not clear what the will is and how it operates, if not dependent on the mind or the body. Moreover, the picture of choice given by the existentialist is faulty, for we do not come into a situation where all options are equally open. Rather, we come from a tradition and enter into a tradition. We are part of our heritage and we cannot choose anything at all. The very terms of choosing and the notion of choice stem not only from ourselves, but from others as well. Even if will were the source of morality, we all know the experience of St Paul related in Rom. 7. We may know what is good and want to do it and what is evil and will to resist it; yet often find ourselves doing what we ought not to do and failing to do what we ought.

The prescriptivist does not escape from criticism. It is doubted whether we can choose or will that anything at all be good or bad. But this is nonsense. Some areas of life are known to be genuine moral areas, while others are nothing to do with morality. Morality is more than mere prescription. It also depends on description.

It is now time to reflect on our map. If you have been following the last section, it is obvious that the neat categories of experience and will are in no sense water-tight compartments. Prescriptivism clearly depends on reason as well as the will. But this is to move into the realm of the detailed study of the moral map. We have tried to avoid too much of that so that we might see the broad lines of importance in a sketch of morality. There are clusters of moral theories in our modern world which do centre on reason, or on sensation (experience), or on will as *the* fundamental source of and basis for morality.

There is, however, another respect in which our map falls short. Sketched as it is, it fails to mention one or two important lines of moral thought today. In order to give a more complete picture of modern moral themes, we need to examine one further key approach, that of the sciences and reductionism.

5   The sciences and reductionism

Perhaps the most significant change in the last century has been the impact of science on the world. By science we are referring to all the sciences. In the previous chapter we saw something of the way in which scientists have become the priests of the modern age. Scientists are the ones who understand the mysteries of life and the world and are able to work miracles today. This is not only true in the physical sciences but is also the case in the biological, psychological and social sciences, at least as far as many people are concerned. The scientific practitioners themselves are much more cautious and are only too well aware of their own limitations and those of their sciences. Yet popular opinion has given great credence to scientific claims and among such claims there are some with direct implications for morality. To show how this operates we turn our attention to *Teaching Christian Ethics* (ACCM Handbook, SCM 1974), which is a handbook designed to help those teaching ethics in theological colleges.

In the introduction, a number of 'scientific' approaches to morality are described and evaluated critically. Each view is to be measured against a particular question: 'Does this account for man's moral experience, his obligations, ideals, strivings and moral emotions?' (p. 4). There then follows an account of the biological, psycho-analytical and sociological views of morality.

(1)   THE BIOLOGICAL VIEW
The emphasis on biology claims to explain the genesis and direction of morality. It tries to tell us where morality comes from and where it is going. It stresses what is natural. It operates on the basic view of man as the product of random mutations. It stresses that instructed behaviour patterns govern human behaviour. Morality is not a distinctively human endowment. Morality does not give man any unique dignity. Human life is the same as animal life. Morality is about the behaviour patterns which contribute to the survival of the species. What we call moral obligation is really

the sense of inhibition which arises at the thought of breaking behaviour patterns which contribute to the survival of the species. In this way, morality is not a rational matter. It is purely instinctive and functions on behaviour patterns and our responses to them. It might be possible, however, to construct a rational morality by using codes of behaviour which tended to the survival of one's own kind. In this way, survival of the fittest or intensification of consciousness are the sorts of things which are right. Indeed, to say that something is right is to say that it is in accordance with nature or that it is conducive to survival. The only motives people have for doing what is right are animal fear and the desire to survive.

There are some basic problems with this view. It is not clear what is natural. Are we thinking here of the level of molecular biology or of chemical interaction? Is natural to be defined by what happens in the jungles of South America or middle-class suburbia in Scandinavia? Moral ideals seem very common, yet animals do not and cannot have them. Are they therefore to be dismissed? If we do take this view seriously we are accepting that things like lust and aggression are normal, natural and good. Surely this is contrary to common sense. Such an account would open the way to biological engineering and manipulation. This would call in question people's freedom. Is it true that all moral rules are aimed at survival, and is it possible to reduce all moral rules to biological terms? The main problem with such a biological account of morality is that it is reductionist and reduces morality to biology. Such a reduction goes too far, for in removing freedom, will, choice, and love for others, what kind of morality is left?

(2) THE PSYCHO-ANALYTIC VIEW

A classic example of this theory rests on the Freudian account which 'stresses the unconscious motivations of much human behaviour, and gloomily reduces the basic human emotions to those of sexuality, fear and aggression'. The heart of the Freudian method is analysis which, in its many forms, encourages men to recognize their most basic motives. Though the analyst insists that morality is not his concern, in practice many repressive moral inhibitions are released in this way, and there is a tendency to regard '"conscience-morality" as repressive, infantile, irrational and destructive of true self-knowledge and integrity'. On this account, 'morality consists of a set of inhibited acts and emotions, and ideal self-images. . . . Men act morally because their super-egos remain strong, binding forces which no mere reasoning can overcome.' *Teaching Christian Ethics* offers this summary of the psycho-analytic view:

(1) Morality is explained in terms of its genesis in infantile experience;
(2) The process is explicable solely in terms of psychological forces . . . ;
(3) The content of morality (what is prohibited) may arise by the mechanism of association, so that one is unable to do certain things because they come to have a quite non-rational association with some object of fear or hatred.

Such an account of morality runs into a number of problems. The main attack follows the genetic fallacy. Such a fallacy is to imagine that, when we have explained how something started, we have fully explained what it is now. Even if the psycho-analytic view does explain the genesis of moral feelings, it does not therefore prove that this is all there is to morality. The psycho-analytic approach rests on strong subjectivist, even hedonist lines. But it is not the case that to say, 'You ought to do something' is the same as, 'You really do want to do that something in the long run'. Indeed often our desires conflict with social justice and this raises moral dilemmas. To accept this explanation of morality would be to change fundamentally our notion of explanations. The Freudian claims that he is able to explain what is inexplicable. But is his explanation plausible? If he is correct and does understand us all better than we understand ourselves, then perhaps we should pass all decision-making and power over to him. Then who would guard the psycho-analytic guardians?

(3) THE SOCIOLOGICAL VIEW
As a key example of the sociological view of morality the Marxist account is examined.

The important points concerning morality here are: (1) There are no universal, absolute moral laws. One's 'moral' beliefs are historically and socially conditioned, and vary from one era or class to another; (2) Moral beliefs are not 'true' or 'false', 'correct' or 'incorrect'. One's moral values arise from one's social position, and from the social structure, and simply express basically socio-economic conflicts or standpoints. They either justify one's class-position (the value of tradition) or attack superiors (moral reform) or compensate for an unsatisfactory social position by providing an 'inner arena' for success (other worldly, personal morality). When the class structure disappears, morality will disappear with it, for truly free social relationships will eliminate the need for such ideological super-structures.

Basic doubts may be raised about the viability of the Marxist account on the grounds of whether the statement of the Marxist position itself escapes from the social conditioning it propounds for all ideas. Some argue that believing what is right makes people challenge the rules and values of their society, rather than simply acquiescing in social norms. Besides which, there does seem a realm of personal morality which may be distinguished from social conventions. Others have suggested, as against relativism, that because men share the same basic human nature, there are some universal moral norms like rules against murder, theft and lying. These laws, it is held, cut across societal and cultural differences.

(4) REDUCTIONISM

The importance of these last few views is that modern scientific accounts derived from biology, psychology and economics do offer an alternative account of morality. The essence of all these views is *reductionist*. They all seek to reduce morality to some one simple basic ingredient whether that ingredient is animal behaviour, human psychology, or economic processes. Morality and man are reduced to one aspect of human experience. In this sense the scientific approaches go hand in hand with the earlier attempts to characterize the basic source of morality in the realm of thinking, feeling or volition.

Our response to all is to express an unease about all such reductions. It seems that, whenever someone tries to reduce morality, he leaves out some crucial and fundamental part of ethical life and practice.

The aim of this chapter has been to outline some of the important values that surround us today. At the same time we have tried to show some of the critical responses which the thinking person ought to make. We need now to move from this general level of values in society at large to the specifically Christian realm of values. At the same time, Christians are not immune from the world in which they live nor from the values that surround them.

3
Christian Values

The intention in this chapter is to examine the sources of Christian moral principles. These sources may be quite independent of the way we *apply* and *use* these principles in moral decision-making. Before we examine how they are used and ought to be used, we need to know what are the moral principles.

1   The divided mind

The dictionary definition of schizophrenia is 'mental disease marked by disconnection between thoughts, feelings and actions'. On this definition most Christians are schizophrenic. There is a mental dis-ease for many Christians. They live in two distinct worlds which often appear totally disconnected. Christians are modern people too. They inhabit the modern world. They are affected by the world in which they live. They are influenced by the values that surround them. They are twentieth-century people, thinking twentieth-century thoughts and living twentieth-century lives. In their work and homes, they function as well as anyone else. They sit and pass examinations, get promotion, and succeed in business and commerce. They look exactly the same as their non-Christian neighbours and workmates; yet they claim to be different.

Christians are different in the sense that they believe certain things that most other people do not believe. If this was a book about Christian doctrine, we would examine some of the central doctrinal beliefs which distinguish Christians from non-Christians. However, there are other differences, often linked to doctrinal beliefs, but which are essentially differences in value. In fact, the difference in morality may not be so much the values themselves but rather the way Christians arrive at their values. This difference of approach needs to be made clear because we live in a post-Christian era, where much of our social and even our personal morality in the West is recognizably Christian in content. Most of the moral principles we hold dear are derived from Judaeo-Christian teaching. This does not mean that most of us believe in and accept these moral principles because they are Christian. Christianity is the route by which these principles have come to us, but we accept them because we think they are right and good, and because we are not convinced by the alternatives. This is the 'genetic fallacy' defeated. The fallacy is to imagine that because you have explained the origin of something, you have totally explained what it is now. Simply because most people's moral principles arose from Christian teaching, does not mean that they are now based solely on Christian thought. Christians are different, not so much in their moral principles, but in the way they arrive at those principles.

There have been different reactions among Christians to this kind of difference. Some Christians have failed to notice the division between Christian values and secular values. Their situation is rather like the man sleeping in his tent, who is disturbed by his camel asking if he might put his nose in the tent. The man agrees and tries to go back to sleep. The camel complains that he is still cold and wants to put his head in the tent. Gradually there is more and more camel and less and less room for the man in the tent. Secular values have imperceptibly eroded and replaced Christian values and some people have not even noticed the difference. Other Christians have noticed the difference and have been appalled. To them has fallen the task of fighting against the erosion of Christian values in society and in the Church. They have tried to offer a critique of the modern world and the secular values it espouses, at the same time as proclaiming Christian values and the necessity to hold fast to these values. A prime example of this tactic is the Nationwide Festival of Light organization. In its disquiet at the moral degeneration of our nation, it has mounted a legal and publicity campaign against pornography in every shape and form. It has been active in lobbying parliamentarians, writing to the press, and organizing rallies and meetings to combat the replacement of Christian values by secular ones. The supporters of NFOL are pleading for a return to genuine Christian values and for the maintenance of the distinctiveness of the Christian way of life.

In contrast, however, there are those who have noticed the difference and rather than fight to maintain the distinctions, have attempted to bridge the gap. These are the people who believe that we are indeed modern men and women and that it is no service to the gospel and to Christian values, if we try to hold ourselves at a distance from the modern world. In fact, Christians have a great deal to learn from the modern world and modern knowledge. Christians need, therefore, to adapt their traditional approaches and understanding to fit in with contemporary ways of thought. Bultmann's approach to theology is a good example of this. Bultmann believed that the existentialist had properly diagnosed the situation of modern people. He argued that Christians should accept that diagnosis of inauthenticity and the need for authentic choices. In this way, the Christian could communicate the true essence of the gospel. The problem for the Christian was that the Bible was written using myths or stories which expressed the writer's intention, without actually being themselves true. The task of the Christian was to demythologize the Bible. This was to remove the mythical layers of the stories, so that we might arrive at the heart of the gospel message. This heart was the secret of how to live an authentic life before God. Once the Christian had discerned this essence (the Kerygma) he must use modern expressions and philosophies as the means of communicating the gospel truth to modern people. Rather than struggle with the modern world, Bultmann gladly embraced it as the means of making the gospel and Christian values relevant to people today.

The reactions of the NFOL, Bultmann, and the Christian caught unaware by the force of secular values, reveal that there is some essential distinction between modern and Christian values. The Christian is, or rather up to now, has been different, not so much in the values themselves, but in the method used to derive those values. In a sense, the very success of Christianity has been partly its undoing. By becoming the dominant ground of moral values in society, its morality has become identified with the modern world and simply been seen as part of that modern world. In fact, there may be some sharp differences in the actual moral content of Christianity and the values of modern life, but that depends on the content of Christian morality. Our concern here is with the form of Christian moral judgements and how Christian moral principles are derived. We shall proceed by outlining the sources of Christian moral teaching and then reflect on some of the problems of each of these sources. This will show the dilemma facing the modern Christian. Can he be both modern and Christian?

2 Using the Bible in ethics

The challenge of 'modern or Christian' is nowhere more acute than in the debate over how to use the Bible. At this point, it is enough to say that all Christians use the Bible in ethics in one way or another. It is for this reason that we select the Scriptures as the model for analysis. How people view the Bible in our modern world and how they use it is crucial. It is part of what defines a Christian. The Bible is in some sense or other God's Word and has authority. All of us accept some kind of authority in our lives. We appeal to it as a reference point to explain our actions. The idea of a 'final authority' is of something which cannot be questioned. It is the last word to be said. Obviously people's attitude towards the authority of the Bible varies from unquestioning acceptance to sceptical rejection. The Christian believes that Scripture has something to say to the world and to mankind and that something carries authority. However, biblical authority does not rest in the pages of the Bible itself. This is no paper-Pope. Biblical authority stems from its relationship with God. The exact nature of that relationship is hotly debated. In what sense is the Bible the Word of God? Is it *the* Word of God or does it contain the Word of God? Is it the only Word, or the most important one? No matter how we respond to these questions, it is clear that Christians do use the

Bible in their moral decision-making. The Bible is a source of Christian moral principles and plays an authoritative role in Christian moral decisions. Such a view assumes the possibility of revelation. This is obviously an area of debate with philosophy, but if we assume that revelation is possible, and Christian ethics certainly does that, how are we to interpret the revelation of God in Scripture?

In looking to the Bible to provide moral principles, we are confronted with a wide variety of material. There are comments, warnings, suggestions, insights, prohibitions, principles, laws, examples and much more. To understand what these different things are and their significance for us, we need to understand what the Bible says and the context in which what is said is said. This means learning to put things in their particular contexts and being able to grasp the depth and breadth of biblical meaning. Fortunately biblical scholars provide much of this material in commentaries. They help us to understand what the Scripture is saying. However, this is just the very point at which the serious problems begin. Even if it is true that we can discover what is actually being said in the pages of Scripture, that still leaves open the options concerning what we should do with this. There are a variety of options open to us and these may be described in general terms.

(1) THE TEXT DOES NOT MEAN WHAT IT APPEARS TO SAY

This view suggests that many translations do not make sense. Therefore we ought to look for other ways of expressing the true meaning. For example, when Paul talks of the necessity for women to be silent in Church, we tend to think that means that women ought not to preach or lead services. There is another way of translating this prohibition on speaking. It is that Paul really meant to stop women chattering. Thus, when we come to Scripture, we must judge its sense not simply from the words themselves, but also in light of our modern thinking. If Paul, or any other biblical writer, does not appear to make sense to us, we are free to, and indeed must, correct the text. In this way, we are the standard by which the meaning, sense, and acceptability of the text are to be judged, within the broad limits of all possible translations.

(2) THE TEXT MEANS WHAT IT SAYS, BUT IT IS WRONG

The previous view is taken a stage further in this second approach. Here it is freely admitted that the biblical writers wrote and meant exactly what it appears. But by any reasonable standard today we must reject such views. No reasonable person can accept such views today. Here it is clear the way that modern values are being used to pass judgement on biblical values. The validity of biblical teaching is to be judged by modern man and culture. This, of course, opens the door to relativism. If our world and our outlook change, so too must the significance and relevance of the biblical principles for us.

(3) THE TEXT MEANS WHAT IT SAYS, BUT IT ALL DEPENDS ON THE CONTEXT

The biblical writers were men of their times. They wrote in a particular setting to the problems and people who lived in a definite historical context. Their attitudes, outlooks and beliefs were those appropriate to people of their time, but are irrelevant as a direct guide for our behaviour today. This is not to deny the worth of the scripture material. It offers great insight into the problems facing the people of God in Old and New Testament times and into the minds of the leaders responding to the issues of their day. It is a fascinating piece of historical documentation which provides a clear picture of those days.

This is to deny any claim to uniqueness for Scripture. The Bible, like any other document from the period, provides an interesting source of historical knowledge. Thus there are no absolute principles which may be derived from Scripture, according to this view. This kind of view seems remote and academic, for it does not seem to affect us directly. This is not the case with the next view.

(4) THE TEXT MEANS WHAT IT SAYS, BUT IT MAY MEAN SOMETHING DIFFERENT TO ME

All the Bible was written from a point of view. The writers were expressing themselves and their own experiences. They use pictures and ideas which are foreign to us. Nevertheless, the experiences behind their words are universal and human. It is possible and necessary for us to go behind the myths, ideas and words of the passages, to the writers themselves and their intentions. This exercise will bring us face to face with genuine human experiences.

Such a view stems from existentialism. 'I' am the centre of the universe, which is my universe, the only universe. Meaning, sense, relevance and truth become totally dependent on me and my subjective reaction. My experience is the standard for everything else. If I do not experience it, it is not real. Biblical material is simply an aid to me to do my own thing.

(5) THE TEXT MEANS WHAT IT SAYS, AND IT MUST BE OBEYED LITERALLY

In sharp contrast to the subjective stress of the previous view, this approach stresses the objective nature of biblical truth. There is no escape from the words and their plain, straightforward meaning. If this is the Word of God, it is to be obeyed. To hesitate or deviate, we reject not simply God's Word, but God Himself. This is literalism. The Bible is to be accepted at face value in its obvious meaning. Such an approach offers an absolute authority and seems to provide a definite and simple solution to biblical interpretation. Whether or not such a view can be propounded consistently, or whether its practitioners 'cheat' by using subtle methods of interpretation when it come to 'difficult' passages, remains to be seen.

(6) THE TEXT MEANS WHAT IT SAYS, BUT WHAT IS CRUCIAL IS THE BASIS OF THE TEXT

When the biblical writers set down this message, they did so on the basis of particular theological principles. The passages themselves often reveal these principles. Situations may change, but the principles do not. They are eternally relevant. Our task as Christians is to apply biblical principles to the different situations in which we find ourselves. For example, in 1 Corinthians 11, Paul is giving advice about decorum in public worship. The specific advice he gives is couched in a number of different lines of argument:

a. Keeping the tradition (v.2)
b. The theological pattern of relationship between God, Christ, man and woman (vv.3–4)
c. Feelings (v.6)
d. The theological purpose of man and woman (vv.7–8)
e. Created order (vv.9–12)
f. What is fitting (v.13)
g. What is natural (v.14)
h. Current practice among Christians (v.16)

The supporters of view 6 urge that we try to apply these theological and moral principles to the new moral dilemmas of the twentieth century.

(7)   THE TEXT MEANS WHAT IT SAYS, BUT THAT MUST BE PUT ALONGSIDE ALL THE OTHER THINGS THE BIBLE SAYS

The biblical writers were not trying to answer all the questions that might ever be asked. Nor were they producing a textbook for believers. They were writing to different people in different places. As a whole, Scripture offers us God's revealed Word. Our Christian responsibility is to search the whole of Scripture and weigh each part in keeping with every other part. One part will help us grasp another part. We are to balance Scripture with Scripture, doctrine with doctrine, one truth with another truth. If we want to understand the Bible's view of male and female, we do not focus attention on I Cor. 11—14 and 1 Tim. 2 without looking at Gen., Prov., Eph. 5, Col. 3 and 1 Pet. 3 as well. This view attempts to be faithful to Scripture in its entirety. It accepts that there will be tensions, incompleteness and rough edges. Yet it remains committed to Scripture as a whole.

Some have suggested that these various views fall into two broad categories. The distinction rests on the basis of relationship to Scripture itself. Views 1–4 do not *sit under* Scripture. Views 5–7 attempt *to sit under* Scripture and its final authority. Regardless of whether this is the case, for any of these views to function properly they must all be applied by faithful interpretation of the biblical passages in their literary, cultural and theological contexts. Then, and only then, is it possible to apply the Bible to our present situations.

We have argued that all Christians do use the Bible in the making of moral decisions. This centrality of the Scriptures is not necessarily a point of dogma. It may arise because of dispute over the alternative sources of Christian principles, for example, tradition, doctrine or natural law. While, as we have seen, there is great disagreement as to *how* the Bible is to be used in ethics, there is contrastingly general agreement *that* it is to be used. In the cases of natural law and tradition, there is not only disagreement between Christians as to how these shall be used, but also whether they ought to be used at all. The situation with appeals to doctrine is more complicated, for doctrine does not rest on nothing. In the end, it has roots in tradition, natural law, Scripture or some other form of revelation or understanding. Thus doctrinal expressions rest on things like Scripture and tradition and indeed interact with them. In seeking to look at the sources of Christian principles, it is easier to move from the areas of agreement to those of disagreement. That the Bible is to be used is not really disputed. How it is to be used, of course, is another matter.

3 The sources of Christian values within the Bible

Given that we do want to take the Bible seriously or feel that this is a proper way of proceeding for Christians, we shall soon discover different kinds of writings and themes in Scripture. These themes are important for any attempt to find a source for moral principles.

(1) OLD TESTAMENT: CREATION
It is always good to begin at the beginning. Creation is taken as a source of Christian moral principles. Creation rests on God's initiative and depends on God's activity. God created the world and mankind. Thus we are not surprised to find the claim that God reveals something of himself and his nature in the world and the

people he has made. There are various strands in the analysis of creation as a source of Christian values.

i. Natural Law

When we looked at naturalism in the previous chapter, we learned that this might mean a morality based on the nature of things or on the nature of people. In theological terms, this is known as *natural law*. God had built morality into the world and into man's nature. It is possible with the help of God's gift of reason to discern that moral law. It is an objective reality which is part of the nature of things. God has made the world and us in it so that some things are good and right for us and other things are harmful and wrong. What is bad tends to harm us, while what is good helps us to flourish. This goes back to the way things were at the beginning of all things. The picture in Scripture is of a perfect garden called Eden where harmony reigned. The harmony between man and woman, man and nature, man and the animal creation, and within man himself, all stemmed from a proper relationship to God. Natural law is God's law expressed in us and in the world around us.

ii. Man made in God's image

While mankind was created and shares with the rest of creation a common source, yet man is different from the rest of the created order. This is expressed by the picture of man being made in God's image. As a son or daughter bear the marks of resemblance to their parents, so mankind bears a resemblance to the God who created. There are many different attempts to express exactly what 'image' means in relation to man, but in the moral aspects of image it is possible to be simple and direct. To be made in the image of God is to be a responsible being, answerable to God. Indeed some would argue that this is the very heart of what it means to be in the image of God. It is to be morally responsible before God. This implies that man is not free to live in any way he sees fit. There are some patterns of life that are appropriate for the nature and purpose of man.

iii. Conscience

Some have tried to be more specific about the content of being in the image of God. They have pointed to conscience in mankind as the mark of God's image. They argue, following passages like Romans Chapters 1–3, that conscience is the voice of God within us. This 'voice' gives us a direct, intuitive awareness of right and wrong. We are moral beings, and that morality is an internal judgement of good and evil. We know the difference between the two and if we go against our consciences we feel guilt and remorse. We ought to let our conscience be our guide.

iv. Creation Ordinances

There is an approach to the accounts of creation which looks beyond creation itself and the various interpretations of 'image' to actual moral principles. This view suggests that, when we read the Genesis accounts, we are given not only an account of God's creation of man and the world, but also some 'Maker's instructions'. These instructions concern *man and nature*. Man is given work to do in the Genesis account. Man is 'to fill the earth and subdue it'. This is a creation ordinance of God. It is God's command to man to be a steward over nature and to exercise responsible dominion over the natural realm. There are other creation ordinances concerning *men and women* and *man and God*. It is not good for man to be alone. Woman is created because of man's inadequacy. Men and women are to complement each other in their relationship. (This particular creation ordinance is appealed to by Jesus and Paul when they talk about marriage, divorce and the behaviour of the sexes.) Man is created not only to live in harmony with woman but with God. God set limits to man. Man's proper response to God should be one of obedience and trust. This is the creation pattern, but it did not happen quite like that.

v. The Fall

The Genesis account shows that man disobeyed God. The effects of disobedience were disastrous. Mankind lost paradise. Disruption, disorder, chaos, enmity, toil, death and the loss of harmony result. Man falls out of proper relationship with the world, his helpmeet, and his God. The Fall spoils everything. It also spoils the unequivocal value of natural law, the image of God, conscience and creation ordinances as the source of Christian values. The Fall affects all of these so it is no longer clear what the original natural law was, or the essential image of God in man, or that our consciences are not themselves warped and twisted, or that the creation ordinances are possible to keep in a fallen world because of our fallen human nature. We are not debating the historicity or otherwise of the Fall, but emphasizing that the first stand in any attempt to use the Bible as a source for Christian values is the theme of creation. However, the Fall account suggests that the Bible itself recognizes that morality cannot be built on creation alone.

(2)   OLD TESTAMENT: COVENANT AND LAW

With the collapse of the original harmony between God and man, there is a loss of the immediate awareness of good and evil and of the ability to obey God's commands. How then does Scripture solve this problem? We are presented with a covenant God who enters into binding relationships with his people. These relationships are called covenants and, like contracts, there are two sides to a covenant. (Gen. 12.1-17; Deut. 7.7-8; 30.1-10.) God promises to bless the people of Israel, if they will keep his commandments and honour him. If they fail to keep their side of the bargain, then God will punish them. Covenant finds expression in law. The Old Testament pictures God as revealing his standards to mankind by means of laws. The best known set of laws is the Decalogue or Ten Commandments, but this is simply part of a much more complex series of civil, ceremonial and moral laws, contained for the most part in the Pentateuch (Exod. 20; Deut. 5). This revealed law of God consists of statutes and judgement. God mediates his moral demands to his people through the proclamation of his commandments. The law of God is an expression of his nature, his will and his character. The law covers both duties to God and to our fellow men and women. Some have summed up the essence of law in the shortened form expressed by the lawyer who tried to trap Jesus and got the parable of the Good Samaritan as his reward.

> You must love the Lord your God with all your heart, with all your soul, with all your strength, and with all your mind, and your neighbour as yourself (Deut. 6.5; Lev. 19.18; Luke 10.27, NIV)

Law itself is not without problems as a source of moral values. It may be a curse rather than a blessing showing how far short we fall. It may present people with standards which are impossible to keep. Perhaps worst of all, the law may become an excuse for a wrong attitude. The Pharisees found the temptation of legalism too great. The letter of the law may kill the spirit.

(3) OLD TESTAMENT: WISDOM LITERATURE

Proverbs, Job, Ecclesiastes and the Song of Solomon are the source of wisdom teaching. Someone has called the material in these books as 'Laws from heaven for life on earth'. This kind of wisdom is extremely practical and down to earth. It is based on the way things work in the world and stems from experience of how things operate in the affairs of men. There is a wealth of detail on a wide series of practical topics. This kind of morality is the nearest thing in the Bible to worldly wisdom and is often criticized as having little distinctive Christian content.

(4) OLD TESTAMENT: THE PROPHETS

The prophets made no claims to be introducing a new morality. Their aim was to restore the true morality as taught in the law and implicit in the covenant relationship. They tried to recall God's people to God and to ensure that what the people said they believed was put into practice. The prophets wished to restore the original covenant relationship between God and his people. Breaking God's law meant separation, defeat and exile. Keeping God's law meant the opposite. There were a number of distinctive aspects to the prophetic emphasis. They recognized that *religion and morality should go hand in hand*. Israel did not practise what it preached. Religion was a travesty. True religion meant true morality (Hos. 6.6; Amos 5.21-4; Mic. 6.6-8; Isa. 1.11-17; Jer. 6.19-20; 7.22-3). The prophets were powerful critics of dishonesty and social injustice. They attacked those who abused wealth and power in Israel (Mic. 2.8–9; 6.10–11; 3.2–3; Amos; Isa. 5.7 23; Zeph. 3.3; Jer. 7.5–6). The prophets also attacked immorality in passages like Hos. 4 and 6, and in Jer. 7.9; 9.3–6. For the prophets sin was a very serious matter. God must respond to every offence against his nature. This meant judgement. In the book of Hosea we find the whole range of expressions that reveal God's judgement. They are famine (4.19), captivity (8.13; 9. 3–7), war (8.14), death (9.12–16), and the removal of God's presence (5.6, 15). However, there is a positive note in the prophetic moral teaching. It stresses that God's judgement and punishment were designed to bring restoration, repentance and hence forgiveness. The very punishment itself was a sign of God's forgiving, steadfast love (Isa. 9.1–7; Hos. 14; Amos 9.11–15; Zeph. 3.11–20). The prophetic material is a rich source of moral teaching for those seeking to derive such principles from the biblical material.

(5) NEW TESTAMENT: REDEMPTION

If creation is the starting-point for Old Testament ethics, redemption is at the centre of New Testament ethical teaching. The God who revealed himself in creation, in the law and through his prophets, has now fully revealed himself in Jesus Christ, who lives and dies so that mankind might be redeemed. For those who seek a New Testament source for moral principles, it is arguable that they need go no further than Jesus himself. Jesus Christ is the essence of Christian morality.

(6) NEW TESTAMENT: KINGDOM ETHICS

When Jesus came, he brought radical change and transformation. Jesus does not only fulfil all that has been revealed before in creation, law and the rest of the Old Testament. He reveals something totally different. There are a number of ways of expressing this difference. Jesus is *God incarnate*. The previous revelations of moral standards have been abstract. Now they are personified in the God who becomes human. How men ought to live is not merely prescribed. It is lived out in the existence of Jesus. Jesus is also the Messiah who fulfils all the expectations of the messianic hope; yet adds to all that a new dimension. He ushered in the *new Kingdom of God*. This new Kingdom has Christ as its head and means new life and power. It stands in the contrast of light to darkness, freedom to slavery, and God to Satan. This Kingdom has *new laws* and a *new lawgiver*. Jesus is depicted as proclaiming the new laws of the Beatitudes as well as giving a new commandment to his disciples: 'Love one another, as I have loved you'. (John 15.12). The hallmark of the life of the Kingdom is love. This is the *agape* love of god which Jesus embodies in total obedience to his Father's will. It is a life of loving God, our neighbours as ourselves, and one another as Christ himself loved. The Kingdom life is not a do-it-yourself affair, for it is to share in the benefits of Jesus' life and work. By his salvation, healing and restoration, he enables men and women to be transformed and to live the life of God. This Kingdom is partly here and now and partly still to come. Only in the final eschaton will the glorious life we enjoy in Christ be completely fulfilled and perfected. In the meantime, the followers of Jesus are to look for his return and to use their 'talents' properly, for we are all to give an account of ourselves before God. Reward and punishment are to be meted out according to our pattern of stewardship.

In consideration of Jesus as a source of Christian moral teaching, it is clear that there are two main lines of thought. The first is that it is the teaching of Jesus which gives us God's moral standards and to be a Christian is to live a moral life in keeping with the teaching of Christ. The alternative view interprets Christian morality more as identification with and participation in the life of Christ. In this sense, the Christian is so to live like Christ in the world, that he is totally identified with Christ. This imitation of Christ is only possible if we live in complete harmony with God. This is summed up by the apostle Paul's picture of life 'in Christ'. It is important to note that this life in Christ does not refer to a dead Christ, but to participation in the life of the risen Christ, who lives and reigns with God.

(7) NEW TESTAMENT: PAUL'S ETHICS

In turning to the Pauline literature as a source of ethical teaching, we are most conscious that Paul, like the other biblical writers, is *not* writing an ethics textbook. His approach to moral themes is not systematic and we glean his ethical principles rather than find them presented in a consistent way. For Paul theology and ethics go hand in hand. Doctrine leads to the moral life. Thus his teaching about the nature of man and the world and his hymn to the humbled and exalted Lord in Philippians are the bases of appeals to live in certain moral ways. Paul uses the law as a means to arrive at the necessity of Christ's help to live the life required by God. That life is a life of love (1 Cor. 13) and fulfils the law (Gal. 5.14; Rom. 13.8). Paul's ethical emphasis is on a community ethic which caters for the whole person. Imitation is the key to Pauline teaching. We are to imitate God, Christ, the heroes of faith and even Paul himself. Paul lays down both specific patterns of moral teaching and also means of solving ethical disputes. He tells us how husbands, wives, and children, masters and slaves, rulers and ruled should live. He also deals with the topic of moral diversity in Romans 14—15:

a. Be fully persuaded in your own mind.
b. Recognize that you will give answer to God, for all of us are judged by God.
c. Do not cause your brother to stumble or fall.
d. Pursue the things that make for harmony and the growth of one another's character.

(8) NEW TESTAMENT: THE PASTORAL EPISTLES

The problem-centred approach to morality is a marked style in the pastoral epistles. They are written to those in the midst of pastoral situations who require direct advice. The moral teaching is thus central but by the way in the writer's presentation. A vast variety of moral virtues are commended and a host of vices condemned. False teachers, bishops, deacons, men of God, the rich, the young, the aged, and what is good and bad for the Christian are detailed in such books as 1 Timothy and Titus. This is a rich source of moral teaching for those willing to dig deeply.

3a Checklist

What we have now is a checklist to use when we come to the Bible with a specific moral problem. If we want to make sure we have considered what the Bible has to say about an issue, the following list serves as a means of dividing up the material and ensuring that we have covered the whole ground.

(1) *CREATION*: ARE THERE PARTICULAR PRINCIPLES TO BE DERIVED FROM THESE SOURCES?
   a. Natural law
   b. Man in the image of God
   c. Conscience
   d. Creation ordinances
   e. The Fall

(2) *THE OLD TESTAMENT*: WHAT PARTICULAR PRINCIPLES MAY BE DERIVED FROM THESE SOURCES?
   a. Covenant and law
   b. Wisdom literature
   c. The prophets

(3) *THE NEW TESTAMENT*: WHAT PRINCIPLES MAY BE DERIVED FROM THESE SOURCES?
   a. Redemption
   b. Kingdom ethics
   c. Paul's ethics
   d. The Pastoral Epistles

We have spent a good deal of time examining the use of the Bible in ethics. This is quite deliberate, for the main ground of Christian moral teaching has used the Bible as the means of discerning God's will for mankind. Scripture alone, however, is not the only source of Christian moral teaching.

4 Tradition as a source of moral teaching

All branches of the Church have appealed to historical precedents in support of their particular denominational, doctrinal or moral emphases. Within the Catholic way of the Church there has been a consistent use of tradition as a proper ground for Christian moral teaching. This is no surprise given the insights to be gained from traditional formulations of Christian moral principles.

Perhaps one of the best ways to illustrate the importance of appeals to tradition is to look at the recent debate over nuclear weapons. It is interesting how both sides in the dispute—which we might characterize as the pacifist and the multi-lateralist options—make clear and direct appeals to the pacifist tradition as found in Scripture, the early Church and the history of the pacifist position throughout the ages and to the tradition of the Just War theory again as it has been propounded and adapted through the changing circumstances of history. Our point is not to make a judgement between these views but to show that regardless of your own view, there is clear appeal and reference to the tradition of the Church both in terms of its interpretations of Scripture and in its historical practice. The same picture would emerge if we examined the current literature within the Roman Catholic Church in the area of sexuality. Both the liberals and the conservatives make appeal and reference to tradition. They may disagree as to how strong a role it should play in the final decision, but they are clear that we cannot ignore our tradition and that of the whole Christian Church.

It is easy to misunderstand such an appeal for it is not simply to the tradition itself, but also to the reality and relevance of the authority behind the tradition. The lessons to be gained from study of the tradition are both positive and negative. They show us the mistakes to avoid, as well as the lessons to be learned.

This examination of tradition as a basis for morality is done through the history of various formulations of Christian ethics. These are interpreted as expressions of understandings of God and Christ. Tradition reflects the experience of the Church. It rests on the validity of generalizations from one situation to another and this is dependent on a common God-given rationality. Often this rationalistic aspect of the appeal to tradition takes the shape of natural law and its examination. Jesus himself built on and adapted the Jewish tradition. Catholic teaching has emphasized the deposit of faith and the necessity to uphold 'true' interpretations of Scripture. Protestants have been less willing to appeal to tradition than to Scripture alone.

We cannot separate ourselves from our traditions and heritage. We enter into life in the midst of a tradition. It helps to make us what we are. Even the questioning of such tradition comes, in a way, from the tradition itself. It would be possible and profitable for us to examine the great moral traditions of the Church from Augustine and Aquinas, through Luther and Calvin, to the great moral theologians of the previous century. What is more vital for our purposes is the realization that such a study of and appeal to tradition rests on the assumption that tradition will provide a solid base for Christian moral teaching. If this is the case, however, the appeal to tradition rests on a more basic appeal to the work of the Spirit in the midst of such tradition.

The Spirit and the Church as sources of morality

The New Testament view of Christian ethics is dependent on the view that God's Holy Spirit dwells in the hearts and minds of Christian believers. This stems from the early chapters of Acts where the giving of the Spirit at Pentecost is described. It is thus that the prophecy of Jeremiah 31 is fulfilled:

> Behold, the days are coming, says the Lord, when I will make a new covenant with the house of Israel and the house of Judah, not like the covenant which I made with their fathers when I took them by the hand to bring them out of the land of Egypt, my covenant which they broke, though I was their husband, says the Lord. But this is the covenant which I will make with the house of Israel after those days, says the Lord: I will put my law within them, and I will write it upon their hearts; and I will be their God, and they shall be my people (RSV).

The Spirit thus comes to write the law of God upon the hearts of men and women. He comes to enable us to fulfil Christ's demands. He is the One who guides, teaches and leads into truth. (John 14. 25-31; 15.21—16.15). The Spirit was the generating power and the inner moral guide of the early Christians. He was the One who produced the moral fruit so clearly spelled out in Gal. 5. The Spirit functions in the context of the Church, as may be seen from the

Council in Jerusalem in Acts 15 which met to consider the appropriate moral demands to be made upon Gentile Christians. The Spirit is the moral guide and mentor par excellence, but that has led to the necessity of checking individual claims to be moved and directed by the Spirit. The early Church produced various tests for the presence and activity of the Spirit in a person's life. All these tests centred on the community of God's people, the Church.

The Church as a source of morality

The work of the Spirit is expressed in the context of the Church, though some would argue strongly that God's Spirit is at work in history and the affairs of all men and nations. To discuss what is the activity of God's Spirit in those settings is much more difficult than in the context of the Church. The Church is the body of believers and is called the new Israel, the Body of Christ, and the community of the Spirit. It is the centre of the Kingdom of God and witnesses to the presence and power of the Kingdom in the world. Because the Church exists in the world it is shrouded in ambiguity by being in the world yet not belonging to that world. It calls its members from the world yet sends them into it. The Church is called to mediate the judgement and the mercy of God. It is to condemn evil in the world and to proclaim the Good News of God. Thus the Church exists for ministry and mission. It is to incarnate the values of Christ. Its members are to live the Christian life.

When the Christian is called to pass a moral judgement on modern issues where there is no biblical teaching and no experience to draw on from tradition, he is not helpless and left with nothing to say. The Christian then, in particular, looks to the work of the Holy Spirit to guide and direct his thinking, so that the will of God in the new situation may be discerned. Such a procedure would soon reduce to subjectivism and be affected by personal preference unless there was some means of checks and balances. The Church as the community of God's people provides that series of checks and balances, for the Spirit guides and directs in relation with and in the context of the whole people of God. This is why many free churches have built their forms of church government and ordering on congregational lines. This is an attempt to discern the will of God by the Spirit in the context of the Church. In essence, this is little different from the Catholic notion of the 'agreement of the faithful'. A helpful picture suggested by Robert Murray of Heythrop College describes what this might mean. Cricket is a game which has laws and yet it is not the laws which are the essence of the game. The game depends on people's attitudes and playing the game in a particular way with the right kind of spirit. It is remarkable that, despite the great cultural differences between Australia, the West Indies, India, England and Pakistan, there is nonetheless an essential agreement about how the game should be played. There is something far deeper than written laws and codes of practice. It is an international, cross-cultural agreement as to what is and should be the essence of good cricket among the cricket faithful the world over. This is how the Church should be at its best, and such unity of thought and attitude would be a powerful and perhaps convincing mark of the presence of God, as well as a source for Christian responses to new moral challenges in our modern world.

Living with the divided mind

There is a tension between the world in which we live and the values that surround us, on the one hand, and the Christian sources of values enshrined in Scripture, tradition, the Spirit and the Church. The nature of the modern world poses fundamental questions for each of these sources of values. Critical scholarship and its fruits as well as the pressure from cultural relativism pose basic questions about the Bible. How can there be such a thing as revelation? How does it operate in relation to Scripture? What is the inspiration and authority of Scripture? What relevance does biblical teaching have to the modern world? Are we not in danger of having a paper-Pope? Tradition, too, comes under fire, for how are we to judge tradition? What standards are we to use and whence are they derived? What relevance has tradition? How may we apply tradition? What are we to do when tradition seems in conflict with biblical principles and teaching? The Spirit and the Church too are open to question, for they may simply safeguard against individual subjectiveness by replacing it with group subjectivity or group preference. What is the Spirit and how does he operate? Can there be a Trinity and, if there is, how does that function? The Church seems an unlikely source of morality for it has been and remains guilty of outrageous actions in the name of Christ and of religion. Besides which, the Church is itself marked by such a degree of variety and diversity that it cannot offer a single clear lead on any moral issue. Perhaps the fiercest charge against the Church is the great gap between what it teaches and preaches and how Christians actually live. The evidence of lives lived seems to count against the genuine moral basis being discovered in the context of the Church.

Conclusion

It is vital that there should be some attempt to answer these questions and the many other criticisms which are brought against Christian values and their location in Scripture, tradition, and the Church. Yet our aim is to see that there are still claims to be able to arrive at Christian values from various sources. These claims continue to be made in the world in which we live and despite the alternative moral values that surround us. We are still left with the basic problem of making Christian moral decisions. Given that now we understand something of our modern world and the popular lines of moral thought which challenge Christian values, and that we still lay claim to be able to discern moral principles in Christianity, we must now turn our attention to *method*. How are we to apply these principles to the real world in actual decision-making? What are the methods of decision-making which Christians may use legitimately today.

4
The Approaches to Decision-Making

In this chapter we shall try to see how Christians have approached the making of moral decisions. Obviously we shall speak in general terms showing the central emphasis in different approaches. There follows discussion of legalism and casuistry, situation ethics, personalism, and what Philip Wogaman calls methodological presumption. Finally, an alternative method of approach will be presented as a *practical* contribution to moral decision-making.

1 Legalism and casuistry

We have described how at the root of Christian ethics lies the concept of revelation. In the moral realm that revelation has been expressed in two ways. There is *general* revelation and *special* revelation. Broadly speaking these categories may be reduced to natural law and Scripture and the Spirit. Natural law has two distinct, yet related, components. It may refer to the nature of the world or to the nature of humankind. In the discussion of naturalism and of natural law itself, we outlined the way such approaches operate. The emphasis is on discerning general moral rules and then applying them to moral problems and situations. This same emphasis may also go hand-in-hand with a strong stress on special revelation. We have seen how the Scribes and Pharisees fell all too easily into the trap of using the Decalogue and the whole of the Pentateuch as a basis for rules and regulations. The task of the Jewish rabbi was to apply these principles and rules to the real world. There is a telling moment in *Fiddler on the Roof* where a new sewing machine has been purchased in a remote village in Russia. The old Rabbi is called for to say a blessing over the machine. It is a struggle to find a suitable rule and then to apply it to sewing machines. Modern rabbis still face problems over rules and their applications. If I spend the sabbath in Britain and then fly to San Francisco, must I observe the whole of the sabbath that is left there? How do sabbath restrictions apply when crossing international date lines and time differences? This same approach to rules is also found in the way people refer to the sayings of Jesus and the writings of the apostles.

Legalism has come to have a very negative connotation. It may now mean a strict sticking to the rules at all costs. Such a danger is inherent in all rule-based moralities. The rules and the keeping of the rules may become an end in itself and far more important than the people whom the rules are designed to help. In this section, we are trying to give a more neutral account of legalism, which is simply an approach to decision-making by the appeal to rules. This kind of approach leads to what is called *casuistry*. The casuist is concerned with the application of ethical rules to special cases. He tries to weigh conflicting obligations by drawing distinctions and classifying exceptions. Casuistry is the application of the legalistic approach to difficult and new problems. The fact that there are so many new problems facing us makes the life of the casuist a busy one. He tries to codify subsidiary rules to the original rules. In this way he makes the decision-making ever more complex. The more qualifications, exceptions and special factors to be taken into account, the more complex the system of rules required to decide in light of all the factors. This makes life seem like one endless moral decision-making process. The more complex such moral decisions are, the greater the need for expert advice. Indeed, we might argue that the sheer complexity of our modern world and the limited understanding we have of ourselves, our situations and the world in which we live, make legalism and casuistry optimistic dreams. To be able to understand sufficiently well to apply the rules may be beyond human wit. If, however, there is any hope of such insight and understanding, it comes through the expert. The most familiar example of the casuist that we might come across is the lawyer. We might go to him for advice on what seems a simple matter, like making a will. All we have to do is to jot down our general wishes and that will be that. It is not so easy. First, the language we use must take a certain form. Of course, our simple prose will do, but it is better (that is, more legally sound) if it is framed in legal parlance and jargon. The lawyer is at pains to show the possible misinterpretations of what has been said, so we must recast our expressions to guard against misunderstanding. Then the good lawyer will point out a series of possible happenings and, what seem to us, unlikely circumstances, which need to be taken into account. Thus we need to express our intention about what should happen, if x, y and z all come true and a, b and c fail to occur. Making a will is a complicated business. We need legal help for two reasons. The lawyer understands the finer points of the law and also has a great deal of experience of what may go wrong and so is able to help us guard against unforeseen eventualities. No matter what happens, our wishes will be carried out to the letter.

If we hold the view that morality is like the legal world, then we need the assistance of someone who knows the law well and is able to apply the letter of the law to situations. The legalistic and casuistic approach to morality attempts to do just that. It seeks to apply moral rules and laws to the real situations of people. However, this may mean a complex set of sub-rules and regulations as well as the need for professional advice. There are, however, some more serious criticisms of legalism and casuistry than the obvious practical ones.

If there is an appeal to natural law as the basic ground of ethics, it seems that the actual number of principles and rules may be very few. Earlier it was argued as a response to relativism that what seemed like fundamental differences between ethical standards in Taunton, Tiree and Timbuctu were examples of the same moral principle. That was concern for one's aged relatives. Unfortunately, even if this is true, it may not be very helpful. To give people a rule—'Do your best for your aged relative'—does not deal with specific ways of doing what is best. The rule is general and vague. Indeed, it might seem so vague and so general as to be singularly unhelpful as a guide to the actual treatment of aged relatives. To appreciate this we need only recall the differences between the three places and what happened to the relatives there.

Such general laws and rules, or even very specific ones, do not cover every case. This is particularly true, and as in the case of the appeal to tradition, the search among the natural laws of Scripture may not give us specific directions for dealing with modern dilemmas. The moral problems caused by eugenics, nuclear power and inflation are far removed from most of the rules we are likely to find in the Bible and in natural law. Indeed, as we come to Scripture or to natural law we have to recognize that rules and laws are conditioned by circumstances. They are propounded in a particular context and were presumably rules fitted for that context and situation. This makes the application of such rules to different circumstances, contexts and situations something that must be argued for on the merits of each case. In practice of course we find that there are some rules we apply and others we neglect. We do not stone witches, cut off our hands nor tithe our yearly crop of herbs or flowers. Yet we do believe that it is wrong to commit murder and right to act as a peacemaker. This shows that the appeal to rules, whether biblical or natural, in itself is insufficient. We need some principle of judgement by which to decide which rules are applicable and which are not, as well as to the universal or relative importance of such rules.

Many of our moral problems seem most acute when sets of rules conflict. In the extreme case of a pregnant woman who will die if her pregnancy continues, we have one principle of the preservation of life. The problem is whose life is to be preserved, given that both cannot be saved. More acutely, we might be in a situation where we have borrowed a gun from someone to shoot rabbits. Late one night, the gun owner demands his gun back. He has discovered that his wife has been unfaithful and, mad with rage, intends to shoot her. Should we keep our principle of returning what we borrow, or keep that of preserving life? Of course, we will try to argue him out of the situation, and it is an extreme and unlikely tale. Yet it shows that in extreme situations (perhaps this is part of what makes them extreme), rules and laws may conflict. Legalism and casuistry on their own do not tell us which rule is to have priority.

The heart of the legalist case depends on keeping the rules, yet this very bold statement embodies some of our unease at the casuist approach. Morality is far more than a keeping of the rules. Indeed we feel that a person whose life is spent living according to the rule book is less than complete. That is the approach of the novice and learner. In the moral life, as on the sports field, we look for flair and freedom. The truly responsible person does not look up the book of instructions about what to do in certain situations. He responds to the need of the moment in light of his principles and aware of the consequences. Such a rule-keeping approach seems a minimal requirement of ethics rather than the fullness of the ethical life. It can too easily encourage the attitude of legalism, in its negative sense, where I fulfil the letter of the law and feel justified. The picture that springs to mind is of the righteous Pharisee struggling to fulfil the six hundred plus rules and regulations of the Jewish law. We can hear him say, 'I managed over five hundred today. Less than two hundred to go'. Paul was at pains to stress that the letter can kill while the Spirit brings life. Rule living may stunt growth, development and maturity.

The final criticism of legalism and casuistry is that in themselves they tell us nothing about the motives for keeping the law. Jesus showed that what happens in a man's heart is as important as the external action. The existentialist lays similar stress on intention as the key to true moral living. The legalist position does not deal with the question of motivation, nor indeed with the moral concern for consequence. Morality is not simply a matter of what we do, but it is also a matter of why we do it and what its results will be. Consequences are morally significant and the keeping of rules in itself does not take account of this. The rule-utilitarian tries to remedy this state of affairs. He argues that we keep the rules, because they lead to the greatest happiness of the greatest number. The Christian legalist would likewise argue that we keep the rules because God has revealed the rules. The danger here is that we become unthinking automatons keeping the rules in some vain attempt to please God, or for fear that we shall be punished if we break the rules or fail to apply them. This conflict is well typified in the writings of the Apostle Paul to Jew and Gentile struggling to gain a proper balance between grace and law, or the Spirit and the law. To the Galatians, Paul used the picture of the two different life styles of the man under the law and the man under the control of the Spirit. The law itself did not and could not bring a person to God, as Paul said of himself in Philippians 3. The grace of Christ with the unmerited favour of God is the heart of Christianity. Our response in humble, thankful obedience and love to that grace is more the essence of Christian morality than legalism and casuistry. Yet rules and their application to situations have their place. This is even the case in what is called situation ethics.

2   Situation ethics

Like so many moral theories, situation ethics arose as an alternative to other approaches to decision-making. Legalism and antinomianism are rejected by Joseph Fletcher, the chief exponent of situationism. Fletcher's rejection of legalism would follow the lines of the last section and his attack on antinomianism is that it is anarchic. The antinomian believes that the situation itself will show us what we ought to do. He depends on the There and Then to provide his ethical solution. This is an intuitionist approach. In Christian history, the Anabaptists followed such a line, believing in the 'inner light' of the Spirit to guide and direct them to moral conclusions. The problem was that the conclusions they reached were in sharp conflict with the moral principles of the Lutherans, Catholics and Reformers. Such individualism, subjectivism and the consequent problems of moral anarchy led Fletcher to seek for an alternative.

The situationist enters into every decision-making situation fully armed with the ethical maxims of his community and heritage. He treats those maxims with respect as the illuminators of his problems. Just the same, he is prepared in any situation to compromise them or even to set them aside in that situation, if love seems better served by so doing. Situationism therefore stresses the use of reason as the instrument of moral judgement, and revelation as the source of the ultimate and absolute moral norm of *agape*. *Agape* is the kind of undeserved love that God has for men. Goodness and right are things now in this situation rather than good and right for all time and situations. This leads to the four presuppositions of situation ethics.

Fletcher's view is based on pragmatism, relativism, positivism and personalism. Situation ethics are concerned with the *practical*: what works is expedient and gives satisfaction. Likewise it deals with what is *relative*. It recognizes that human life is fully contingent and that there are no absolutes or perfect situations. Accordingly, we must act in humility for we are imperfect moral creatures. At the same time we *posit* certain propositions on the basis of faith. These may be theological commands or moral maxims. We affirm them voluntaristically and not rationalistically. By this, Fletcher is drawing attention to our inability to prove the belief that we have in God. We cannot offer convincing proof, but we can posit such faith. The essence of ethical procedure is decision and choice. We are unable to verify the decisions we make, but we are able to justify them. The final presupposition puts people at the centre of the moralist's concern rather than rules or principles. Ethics are to serve the person, rather than be the person's master.

Six propositions sum up the actual content of situation ethics. We are called on to apply these six principles if we are truly to follow the demands of *agape* in every situation.

(1) Only one thing is intrinsically good: that is love (*agape*) and nothing else.
(2) The ruling norm of Christian decision-making is love (*agape*) and nothing else.
(3) Love and justice are the same. Justice is love distributed.
(4) Love wills the neighbour's good whether we like him or not.
(5) Only the end justifies the means.
(6) Love's decisions are made situationally and *not* prescriptively. Fletcher's case rests on the plea to take every situation seriously and to calculate carefully how love will be best served in each setting.

What is faintly amusing, but in the end undermining of this position, is the inherent flaw in its presentation. Fletcher pleads for an end to absolutes and to legalism. At the same time he propounds a new (or rather old) absolute, that of love. Love alone is the only intrinsic good. It is the sole norm for decision-making. We simply exchange what are unacceptable absolutes to Fletcher for a more acceptable absolute. He heavily criticizes the legalistic style of the Pharisees and those who are rule-centred. At the same time, he propounds the necessity of four presuppositions for proper decision-making and argues that the actual content of situation ethics consists of six propositions. What else are these but laws or rules to be applied in every situation? Again, one set of rules and regulations is replaced by a different set. If the method raises fundamental problems for Fletcher, so does the actual practice of such decision-making. The initial problem is how we define 'situation'. If I am to apply the moral maxims and practical calculations of my tradition and heritage to calculate what is the most loving thing to do in a situation, I must know where that situation begins and ends. Is it right that I should be spending my time writing this book rather than spending time with my family? There is a specific moral problem and if I am to follow the situationist line I am to try to calculate what is the most loving thing to do in a situation. But when does the situation of 'writing a book' begin and end? Did it begin when the publishers dreamed up the idea of this kind of book? Or was it when I first talked to my editor? Or was it when I gathered the material together? Or was it when I sat down to write the thing? It is also a problem to know when the situation will end. Will it be when I finish my corrections and check the final proof? Will it be when the book is produced, or when the reviewers hack it to pieces, or angry readers complain that I have been of no help, or I collect some royalties? All these moments in the situation are significant if I am to calculate whether it is more loving to write this book or to spend time with the family. Writing may make me happy and proud, bring help to people, keep publishing-houses in business and supply some necessary cash. It may also have the opposite effect from all these. Spending time with the family may bore them and me, cause friction and strife and make us all over-dependent on each other. Or it may have the opposite effect to all these. But I am still not clear where the situation, and so, where the calculation begins or ends.

The same kind of problem arises with weighing up love in terms of consequences. I do not believe that Fletcher is really arguing for moral decisions being made because *we feel* that something is loving. All his talk of calculation puts him directly in the tradition of the utilitarian pleasure-calculator, except it is love which is to be measured rather than pleasure. But how do I know and how may I guarantee certain consequences? Let us look again at the imaginary example cited on page 5. I had every specific intention of murdering the principal of my college and tried to carry out my plan to the very best of my ability, but *my calculations went sadly wrong. I could not foresee the way the consequences would turn out*. Calculating consequences is a hazardous business with little certainty and with the additional problem of knowing when to cease the calculation. Is the sum to be the most loving thing judged at the end of this year, next year, or in thirty years time? The answers may be very different according to when and where we draw the line.

Such a complex operation of calculation and of ensuring that we do justice to the four presuppositions and the six propositions, while grasping the true nature of the situation, makes the task of the casuist look simple in comparison. To be a successful situationist, it looks as if you need to be omniscient and able to withstand the pressures in every situation which make it extremely difficult to be objective and fair. To suggest that 'the loving thing' is an objective standard is implausible, for there is great variety of view among Christians as to what constitutes the loving action. Is it loving to refuse to marry people in church when one or both parties have been divorced? A proper answer to this question needs to ask, 'Loving for whom?' Is it loving for the couple, for their families, for their previous spouses, for people in the Church struggling with difficult marriages, for young people asking whether marriage is for life or not, or for the vicar with a bishop breathing down his neck? Situationism tells us that love is what we need, but for whom?

Finally, from a whole host of possible criticisms, we may ask whether love and justice are really the same thing and if the end always justifies the means. The picture of the law court where justice is dispensed seems far from the contexts where love flows forth. The kind of legal rules we have are minimalist and seek to draw a line below which we will not allow people to fall in their treatment of and relationship with each other. This justice is far removed from love. The law may require that we do not discriminate against those of a different colour or creed. Such laws clearly state that certain forms of behaviour are unacceptable. They are unjust. This negative form is hard to marry with the positive demands of love. The law cannot require of us that we love our racially different neighbours. Such a law could not be enforced. Indeed some might argue that a proper enforcement of such a law would itself be unjust. Justice and love are not exactly the same.

Nor does the end always justify the means. Many have commented on the exceptional nature of the cases which are presented by Fletcher and his supporters. One is right to be suspicious of a morality which is based on the exceptional in life. The exceptional examples may seem to show that the end justifies the means. However, that some ends justify some means, does not mean that all ends are justified by any means. There are surely some means that are so degrading, disgusting, harmful and evil that we would never use them no matter how worthy our cause and the end in view. We would all accept that our children need some protection from bad influences in the world. But we would do well to question the wisdom of using total separation from schools, playmates, television, radio, newspapers, books and other people as proper means of achieving a worthy end. Not all means can be justified by the end.

The criticisms of legalism, casuistry and situation ethics should not mislead us. There are important insights to be gained from both approaches. Moral rules and their application are vital to morality and decision-making. Christian love is central to Christian morality and we must seek to express that love with as full a grasp of the situation as possible. Morality in general, and Christian morality in particular, has not remained stuck with these models of decision-making. We now examine two recent lines of approach to moral decisions.

3 Personalism

Strictly speaking 'personalism' is not a method of decision-making, yet it does sum up a set of moral presuppositions and the way in which they are applied to moral dilemmas today. Thus 'personalism' is the holding of certain moral values which cluster around the notion of personhood and what constitutes growth and development of personhood. These values are then applied regularly and consistently in such a way that it is possible to talk of a distinct approach to moral problems.

The report *Homosexual Relationships* outlines the number of approaches to morality and lists the personalist view as '. . . what matters in sexual behaviour is the quality of personal relationship that it serves to express and confirm' (p.47). This view is widely expressed in the area of sexuality by modern writers. Jack Dominian, a Christian psychiatrist and counsellor, expresses the essence of the view thus: 'All human activity, both intra- and inter-personal, is now seen in terms of enhancing or diminishing the potential of being fully human.' (*Proposals for a New Sexual Ethic*, p.36).

This statement of personalism depends upon the definitions of 'person' and 'love'. Dominian takes care to define both:

> . . . A person is a psychosomatic unity who, from the time of conception onwards, realises his/her physical, intellectual, psychological (affective and cognitive perspectives) and spiritual dimensions within the particular socio-economic matrix of his/her society. The psychological key to being a person is the dynamic concept of *wholeness*, that is to say, having access in a balanced form to all one's dimensions, both conscious and unconscious, and *growth*, a continuous process which allows the realisation of one's potential (p.36).

Thus it is possible for Dominian to summarize the basic essentials of a person as 'the constituents of psychosomatic unity, their integration into a dynamic whole and the growth of the summated potential of the whole' (p.36). For the definition of love, he describes his usage of the term. 'I have tried to specify the meaning of love by using three key words, sustaining, healing and growth, which in turn demand certain contingencies of permanency, continuity and predictability' (p.37).

For Dominian and the personalist in general the test of all human relationships and contacts is very simply stated. 'What really matters is the encounter of persons and the presence of love' (p.58). The cash value of the personalist approach is to judge all relationships, but particularly sexual ones, by the criteria of personal fulfilment and mutuality. It is not a selfish doctrine, but expresses a genuine concern for the other. The strength of the view is also its weakness. It assumes both that we really understand what a person is and what is good and bad for them, as well as knowing (and hopefully controlling) what the consequences of our actions are to guarantee loving, wholesome, growing results. It is difficult to see how we can ensure a loving motive in all that we do. Even if this is possible, it is hard to be certain what the loving results will be of our actions. Persons vary greatly and the personalist approach seems to reduce to treatment of individual cases. As a plea to remember the importance of individuals it is very necessary. It is less helpful as a general guide to what one actually does with these people and how one may guarantee the results of one's actions so that they will lead to the sustenance, health and growth of the person concerned.

4 Wogaman's methodological presumption

The case Wogaman presents in *A Christian Method of Moral Judgement* stems from the tendency in ethics to deal with moral judgement in two ways. The first path is that of ethical perfectionism in which a particular moral tradition supplies the correct answers. There is no uncertainty in this approach. The answers are obvious to the initiated. The other extreme for Wogaman is that of the situationist, who is concerned with the end to be achieved and judges the means by the end. He enters into every situation with no precommitment concerning the best course to follow. The situation will provide the solution, in as much as solutions are possible.

Steering between the Scylla of perfectionism and the Charybdis of situationism, Wogaman introduces the idea of moral presumptions. These are initial biases that we have in decision-making. These presumptions are to be tested in light of the evidence. If there is good ground for rejection, we are to reject the presumptions. If doubt remains, we ought to decide on the basis of these initial presumptions. His basic way of dealing with uncertainty is probably rooted in moral tradition; yet he arrives at judgements which will allow unambiguous action by examining the realms of jurisprudence and legal presumptions, and the decision-making of business executives.

This approach is not novel, argues Wogaman, but is something we all do in practice. He recognizes that our presuppositions are our basic prejudices or prejudgement of the facts. He recognizes likewise the unwillingness of some to test or check their presuppositions. So to do is to be guilty of a lack of moral seriousness and a failure to recognize human limitations. Wogaman then examines moral exceptions and the ways in which it is proper to set aside moral presumptions. He then deals with the 'significant forms of presumption' and 'polar principles', in which he attempts to give some outline of the content of the presumptions, for example, procedural, principle, ideological, empirical and authoritative, as well as the positive and negative moral presumptions of the Christian faith. These Christian presumptions can find expression in the more general polar presumptions of the individual/social nature of man, freedom and responsibility, particularity and universality, conversation and innovation, and optimism and pessimism. These polar presumptions affect all moral decision-making and are not explicitly Christian in content.

It is hard to see how successfully Wogaman has avoided the extremes. His appeal to prejudice as a basic starting point rings oddly, but even if one allows the commonsense support that there must be for such a retreat to prejudgement, it is much more difficult to see how one might get beyond the level of prejudice. Our prejudices are usually deep-seated and often irrational. To use rational means in trying to deal with them may not be entirely to the point. It is hard to see how we might genuinely change our morality on this view. If the response is that change is not the aim, then there must be doubt about the point of the exercise, except as a reinforcement of prejudice. There is no doubt that Wogaman is right to stress the crucial importance of our presuppositions and the way our presuppositional frameworks operate in moral decision-making. Some might query the legal system and the practice of business men as a sound basis for ethical choices, yet we all do have frameworks of operation. Wogaman shows us this, but is perhaps less helpful in showing what we are to do with our framework in the actual making of decisions which seem to be more than a matter of dealing with our prejudices.

5   A method applied: the personal history

It all began when I was asked to teach people how to think. There is a branch of philosophy which purports to do just that. It is called logic. So I designed a course on logic. It was very boring, because it was not the way most people thought most of the time. Thus I began to explore informal logics or ordinary ways of thinking about things and was struck by the way that one particular method had cornered the market. It was called 'lateral thinking'. Edward de Bono had developed this approach to thinking in a desire to encourage creative thinking. He complained that most of our attempts to teach people to think were along vertical lines. We taught people to dig the same hole deeper. Hence the move to increasing specialization and more and more knowledge about less and less. He introduced lateral thinking, which is a formalized name for what many of us do naturally. If one hole doesn't look as if it will produce oil, we drill other holes in likely spots. In other words, we move sideways to try to see the problem in a different light and to try a new approach. De Bono designed a simple way of teaching children how to do this lateral thinking.

At the same time, I was teaching Christian ethics and working in a theological college, training men and women for the pastoral ministry. The range and scope of moral problems was ever increasing. I could teach them the principles from the Bible, tradition, the Spirit and the Church. I could show them how to apply these principles legalistically, situationally, personalistically and by methodological presumption. Yet I was uncertain whether I had taught them how to cope with the moral problems which our modern world will produce in forty or fifty years time. The second problem with the approaches we tended to use was that they carried certain assumptions implicitly and the very assumptions which helped to get the method off the ground became, in the end, a hindrance to arriving at proper moral conclusions.

Thus I began to put my two teaching areas together and what follows is the attempt to do that. There is no novelty in the approach. It is I believe more a setting down on paper of what we do already, than a new moral approach. There are some things which need to be said before we explain the method. These result from comments in various church groups when I have talked about the approach.

6 The method applied: some clarificatory remarks

Rarely do we make moral decisions. Baldly put like this, it feels wrong. Most of the time, however, when we are faced with moral issues or problems, we react. We do not think about the moral dilemma, but simply respond to it. This is not to say that our reaction is immoral or subjective. On the contrary, our reactions are highly moral. They are a reflection of our moral teaching, heritage and tradition. They reflect the ways in which we have been morally educated and trained. In one sense, that we respond to moral situations making moral judgements without a great deal of thought is a tribute to the success of our moral inculcation. We do not need to think about most issues, for our moral reaction comes quite naturally. This is expressed with some care. Our reactions come 'quite naturally' rather than 'naturally'. There may well be some intuitive appreciation of natural law, some inherent awareness of our own nature and what is good and bad for us, as well as the voice and power of conscience, but all of these may be fostered, encouraged and enhanced by proper moral tuition. It does not simply happen if we are left to our own devices. William Golding's horrific account of what does happen in such circumstances is only too real for comfort. *Lord of the Flies* embodies the fear and certainty we have as to what life would be like, if the trappings of civilization and society were removed.

Our reactions, then, are moral, for they are part of our moral teaching, but they are also part of our moral experience. People are far too sensible to carry on believing what does not work in practice. If a method or principle consistently breaks down, we discard it. It is the same with moral principles and methods. If they do not achieve their desired end, we adapt or change them. When we react in a moral situation, we reflect our moral experience and insight. It is the insight and experience gained the hard way in the rough and tumble of life and that too becomes an integral part of us. Our reactions in moral situations are the result of our moral experience and awareness of what works to satisfy our own moral criteria.

Our responses are neither immoral nor are they subjective. The danger is of being misled by the empiricist into thinking that because feelings are involved in morality, that is all that there is to morality. Obviously our feelings are an important part of morality. It would not be morality unless it affected us and our emotions and engaged our feelings. But this is very far from suggesting that we are victims of our feelings. When we react to moral issues, we are not simply allowing our feelings to get the better of us. We are expressing moral attitudes and revealing moral principles. These attitudes and principles are not purely subjective things, but are objective. They do not depend on us for their validity, truth or falsity. We may see this from what happens if someone queries our reaction to a moral problem. Of course, if someone questions our reaction and suggests that it is inappropriate, we may shout, scream and sulk. More commonly, we try to justify ourselves and our reaction. That is to say, we give (or try to) *reasons* for our attitude. We begin to reflect more slowly on what appeared instantaneously. We defend our moral judgements with reasons which we believe will explain and confirm our moral judgement. This appeal to the ground of the judgement will also, we believe, be likely to convince the person who demanded justification of the justice and correctness of our judgement.

To say that we rarely make moral decisions is not the same as suggesting that we never make moral decisions. We do make moral decisions and require a procedure for doing so, but it is much more rare than we imagine. We complained that the situationist made his morality too dependent on the exceptional.

In one sense, he was very near the mark. For most moral situations the old tried and tested rules may be applied without thinking about it. Such decisions are taken automatically. The problem is that every now and then, and only now and then, the rules do not cover the particular example or the law breaks down. Then we are faced with exceptional circumstances. Such exceptions are rare, but do require our moral response. In a sense, we are suggesting that the necessity for moral decision-making procedures arises most actively in a crisis. The crisis is either that the old system will not cope with the problem or that our judgement is criticized and we are called on for justification.

Our usual moral reaction mechanism may not be successful for we may be faced with a genuinely novel problem, a new amalgam of old problems, a conflict between established principles and procedures, or some surprising feature which causes strain on our traditional way of handling the problem. We do not go through all the thinking and checking procedures unless it is necessary. The breakdown and failure of the usual reactions would make this necessary. So too would the demand for justification and our acceptance of the need to justify our actions. In so doing, we would go through some procedure of moral decision-making or rather show how we might have done (or did almost instantaneously). The method that follows is a way of coping with the situations of breakdown or the demand for justification. This demand may even come from ourselves, when something triggers off reflection on a particular action we have taken. 'Why on earth did I behave like that?' may be the first question in a process of seeking justification for our own moral responses.

Some will feel that the approach is too rationalistic. Naturally, it will depend on our ability to reason and apply that reason to real problems. It is not quite clear why people are so 'anti-rational'. In fact, we are rational beings. We are far more rational than we pretend to be, for perceiving, sensing, knowing in physical, psychological as well as moral senses depends on our rational skills. We all use these skills most of the time. Besides, if we hope to have a morality that makes sense from situation to situation and one time to the next as well as from person to person, that morality must be objective. Any attempt to show its objectivity and to present grounds for that view will be expressed in a rational way and depend on our rational abilities to understand words, follow a line of thought and argument, come to a conclusion, and evaluate the whole procedure and the match between the process and the conclusion. To be able to judge what is fitting and appropriate, we need the ability to fit things together and to recognize what is appropriate as well as inappropriate. For those who still protest against rational bias, it is necessary to remind them that this use of the rational faculties will only happen in 'crisis' settings and that the exercise of reason is not here for some abstract purpose, but is designed to be directly practical and helpful. Using our God-given rational faculties does not seem too high a price to pay for being able to cope with moral dilemmas and justify our application of moral principles in a particular situation.

The criticism of the alternative approaches to moral decision-making has made the point that they tend to become prescriptive and affect the content of the judgement, as well as even hindering the judgement in some cases. Only when we have applied our method to moral dilemmas will we be in a position to see whether we escape this criticism. At the moment, it can only be stated that the method is itself a *clarificatory tool*. It is designed to clarify what we are doing, rather than to force particular moral values into our procedures by some process of struggling. This clarification rests on the notion that the approach is essentially neutral. It is a means of helping us make practical conclusions, rather than a set of conclusions itself. Thus critics will complain that there are too few answers. This is entirely deliberate and the basic nature of the method. It is not that there are no answers. Far from it, for in reality the answers are for the reader to arrive at by following the method through to his own conclusions. Our aim is to help others solve their moral dilemmas properly. That is, to be aware of what it is they are doing when they make a Christian moral judgement.

Thus the method, as outlined, is really a setting-down of how people actually make moral decisions if and when they start from scratch. It has been argued that such procedures happen rarely. That does not belittle their importance. We need to know what to do if we are confronted by a new moral issue or some new development in an old problem. The following method is a kind of checklist for how to proceed. In that sense it may seem obvious. It is in the sense that this is generally the sort of thing we do and need to do. .

The method while applying some insights from the work of de Bono has nothing to do with de Bono's views. It is *not* attached to a particular way of thinking or a definite programme for encouraging creativity. Some tools from de Bono may help us in an area in which he would claim no special competence and which is far removed from his own central interests. Even if he is totally misguided, the application of some of his approaches may still be insightful and helpful to us all.

7   The method applied: its content

(1)   CONSIDER ALL THE FACTORS (C.A.F.)

All too often when we make decisions of any kind, we neglect to take some crucial detail into account. This is as serious in morality as in business. It is vital that we consider all the factors. There is a very simple way to begin to do this. It is to have a 'blitz' on a particular topic and jot down everything that we think of as having relevance. The more people there are who do this, the less likely it is that some important factor will be omitted. Often it is helpful to set oneself a basic limit to aim at. 'I will try to list twenty factors that need to be taken into account in this situation.' This sounds more difficult than it is. When we have applied this to some moral issues, we shall soon see it for what it is—common sense.

(2)   FIRST IMPORTANT PRINCIPLES (F.I.P.)

In all decision-making it is vital to get one's priorities right. This procedure reminds us that we have principles and that we need to do two things. Firstly, we need to discover what the principles actually are which are involved in the situation. Secondly, we need to make some ordering of priorities and principles. This is especially crucial if there is likely to be conflict between principles. If it comes down to a choice between principles, which are we to hold to, when all else must go? Some philosophers express this point by saying that it is possible to have only *one* basic and fundamental principle. It is the most basic assumption we make about everything we are and do. It is important to recognize what that principle is and to rank the other principles in order after and in relation to it.

For the Christian, the discernment of the first important principles will proceed as follows:

i. Has Scripture some particular teaching or principles which are relevant here?

This will mean seeking to clarify the theological and moral principles at stake, as well as specific biblical teaching, and reference to other parts of Scripture as a balance and complement to particular passages.

The way we answer the question in detail is by going through our checklist, as set out on p. 58.

ii. Has tradition some particular teaching or principles which are relevant here?

iii. Has the Spirit or the Church some particular teaching or principles which are relevant here?

(3) AIMS, GOALS AND OBJECTIVES (A.G.O.)

It is not enough to be clear what our principles are, we need too to know the aim and direction we are taking. Where do we want to be? What are the objectives in mind? Have we distinguished between what is desirable and what is possible? Perhaps most important of all is to consider what the consequences of my action will be, as far as we can foresee. Can these be avoided or mitigated? In any situation it is important to know the motivation and desires of those involved and the likely consequences of putting their motives into action, by seeking to fulfil their aims.

(4) ALTERNATIVES, POSSIBILITIES, CHOICES (A.P.C.)

It is important to consider all the possibilities and choices open to us in moral dilemmas. There is usually more than one way of responding to a particular problem and first reactions are not necessarily the best. The A.P.C. emphasis involves careful consideration of and reflection on alternatives, seeking to understand the range of options open, before any final commitment to act.

(5) OTHER PEOPLE'S VIEWPOINTS (O.P.V.)

One of the problems with the existentialist approach is that it all too easily degenerates into selfishness. Morality involves taking other people seriously. To do this is to try to look at situations and problems through the eyes of the other people involved. We need only consider the possible benefits of worker seeing with management eyes and vice versa to realize the importance of 'putting ourselves in the other person's shoes'. To consider the problem from someone else's viewpoint means that we cannot simply please ourselves without reference to the wishes and desires of others. Of course, it is not always easy to see things from another person's perspective, especially if we are in initial disagreement with that person. Yet the effort is worthwhile and vital if we are to make a fully informed moral decision. The actual procedure may be expressed visually (see p. 85).

Conclusion

The aim of this chapter has been to offer a description and critique of the popular lines of decision-making among Christians. This was a prelude to an attempt to give some flesh to the commonsense way of making decisions. The method presented is not in itself a moral prescription. It is designed as a clarificatory tool to enable us to cope with the decisions we have to make on the few occasions when such a complex procedure is required. For most of our moral life we are able to rely on our normal moral responses. When these come under fire, or when we are confronted with exceptional circumstances, we do require a method of approaching moral judgements. It now remains to apply this method to some of the moral areas which are in debate for Christians today.

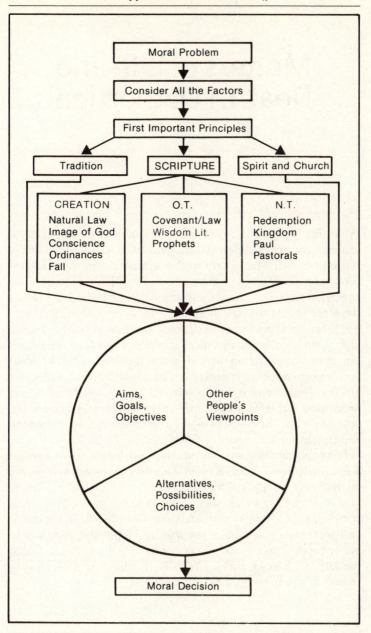

5
Matters of Life and Death: (1) Abortion

Whenever you have a discussion about ethics with medical students, the topics of abortion and euthanasia inevitably come up. It is no surprise, when we realize that it is in these areas the medical profession is under the greatest scrutiny. Recent court cases concerning assisted suicide and the death of malformed babies show the proper concern of a public looking to safeguard society and the medical profession itself. Both abortion and euthanasia are highly emotive issues and there is all the more need for a cool, objective consideration of the issues involved. Our personal involvement with abortion and euthanasia will be rare, unless we are involved directly in the hospital wards or clinics where pregnancy and childbirth or care of the elderly and dying is the normal routine. For most of us, the questions concerning abortion and euthanasia are exceptional and rare.

It is important that we remember our aim here is not to arrive at a particular conclusion. Rather the intent is to show how the method may be applied to a topic in order that each individual or group might arrive at their own conclusions. Our goal is *clarification*, as a means for others to be able to decide. At the end of each section there will be no one answer. Hopefully, there will be greater understanding and clarity concerning the problem, so that the task of decision-making is properly done. It is up to each person or group to do that for themselves.

1   C.A.F. (Consider all the factors)

We need to list the areas involved in the topic of abortion. What are the various aspects of the abortion issue.

a. The mother: her rights.
b. Her health: emotional and physical.
c. Her situation: home, work, relationships, beliefs.
d. The foetus: its condition, its status (is it a person?), its rights.
e. Rights: the mother's, the child's, the father's, the doctors', the nurses', the society's.
f. Law: what is permitted or forbidden? Why is there a law? Does it work?
g. The father: his condition, attitude, beliefs.
h. Moral values: those of the mother, father, medical staff, law, general public.
i. The family pressure: other children, parents and relatives.
j. Public opinion: the media, the local views.
k. Religious beliefs: Church teaching, the Bible, actual practice, her own beliefs, medical staff's beliefs, father's beliefs.
l. Sexual expression: marriage, rape.
m. Economic state: now, after birth/abortion.
n. Prejudices and emotions involved.
o. Doctors' attitude: personal, professional.
p. Nurses' attitudes: personal, professional.
q. Women's Liberation: rights.
r. Definition of life.
s. Definition of a person.
t. Definition and forms of abortion.
u. My involvement in the situation: my role, my beliefs and prejudices, my goal.
v. Consequences of a decision to abort or not to abort: mother, father, family, foetus, medical staff, hospital, National Health Service, society.
w. Who is to choose? Woman, doctor, society, father.

Obviously there will be some degree of overlap but it is important that we focus on the central emphasis of each of the points raised. By the process of 'blitzing' our minds, we can easily come up with this sort of list. The list itself simply gives us the areas to explore. It does not give an order of priority. We shall consider each of a–w in turn making appropriate links and thus simplifying our list of factors before applying the rest of the method, and then checking back to ensure that we have really considered all the factors fully. This may seem like hard work and perhaps even boring. Yet it is vital if we are to grasp the variety of factors at work in the situation and the significance and relevance of these factors for our decision-making.

(a) THE MOTHER: HER RIGHTS

(i) *The woman's rights*
The pro-abortion case may rest on the notion that abortion is every woman's right. After all, it is argued, women become pregnant and carry the baby. Behind this lies the view that a woman has the right to do with her own body whatever she wishes. This may be seen as a basic freedom of womankind. The right of women to abortion on demand is seen as essential to put an end to back-street abortions and the harm they cause. Nowhere is the right to abortion more stoutly defended than in the situation of rape. Today an abortion in such cases is to make the innocent pay for crimes they did not commit. The horrid brutality of rape destroys the dignity of woman. It comes, unwanted, unwelcomed, unlooked-for and undeserved. Is it fair or just to expect a woman to pay the price of evil done to her by forcing or encouraging her to bear the child? Is she to carry the reminder of that awful experience? Is she to be forced to see morning, noon and night the embodiment of what may have destroyed her life, career, opportunities for a loving, stable relationship, and, indeed, herself?

A second strong argument for the right of the woman to have an abortion is the situation where the mother's life is at risk. It is important to stress that such occasions are exceedingly rare nowadays and very rarely is it a direct choice between the life of the mother and the life of the foetus. But the argument does often make the point that, if there is such a conflict, the woman's rights come first. The Women's Liberation Movement, however, is not simply concerned with the exceptional cases of rape or risk to the mother's life. It argues that in every situation, if in the woman's opinion her well-being requires that she has an abortion, her choice is absolute, for her rights are at stake.

(ii) The rights of others (e)

There are contrary views to such an exclusive emphasis on the woman's right. Two lines of argument are presented. The first centres on (e) (p. 102). There are other rights at stake in the issue of abortion and these require exploration. Obviously, the mother has some rights, but so too does the foetus or child. The child is helpless and unable to speak for himself (herself) and to defend his (her) basic right to exist and to be born. If the child is silent, others must speak up on his (her) behalf. The father too has rights. The child in some sense is his and belongs to him. His interests are at stake as well as those of the mother. While recent court decisions have overruled a father's attempt to stop his wife having an abortion, the very fact that the case came to court proves that the law recognizes a prima facie right of the father in such situations. His voice must be heard and his rights safeguarded. The medical staff also have rights. Their own views must be taken into account. They must have the right to refuse to do such operations. This is enshrined in the abortion laws of Great Britain, but, in practice, it may be a different story. The pressure of career prospects, senior colleagues, and the hospital procedures and timetable may force doctors and nurses to act in ways which they regret and find morally repugnant. In such cases, their rights are infringed and ought not to be. Society, too, may have rights at stake. Society may deny that anyone has the right to do whatever they wish with their own bodies. Society may claim the right to prevent people harming themselves and others. Society may claim the right to refuse to allow people to degrade themselves and to cheapen human life.

The second line of argument and debate in relation to the rights of the mother is the area of responsibility. There are no rights without responsibilities. The notion of rights suggests that someone or some group permit or give rights to others. Alternatively, nature itself may endow certain rights, as is suggested in the American Declaration of Independence and the UN Declaration of Human Rights. The having of rights implies the need to perform duties and obligations. In a society, if people have rights they must not abuse these rights and must act responsibly. To do otherwise may be to threaten the existence of the rights and the exercising of such rights. If the woman has rights in the situation of abortion, what responsibilities do these rights carry with them? To whom and for what is she responsible?

In this way we see that there is a *central theme of rights* to be considered. The respective weight that the various claims have, must be measured carefully. (a) and (e) come together and must be considered together, as we have done.

(b) THE MOTHER'S HEALTH: EMOTIONAL AND PHYSICAL

In coming to (b), we see that it is false and unhelpful to separate (b) from (c), (i) and (m)—her situation, family pressure, and economic state. It would also be foolish to fail to refer to (h), (k), (v) and (w); her values, religious beliefs, the consequences for her, and her freedom and ability to choose, as well as her rights. We begin to see the 'blitz' method simply brings out a great variety of themes and material for reflection. It usually can be formed into *clusters*, so that each area will be considered in proper relationship with the others. This is a second-stage procedure, however, and can only happen as we begin to work through the list of factors and begin to realize the inter-relationship. By considering all the factors, we are led to a position where we begin to see the connections between factors and the necessity of considering these factors in concert rather than in isolation.

(i) Emotional health

What is the emotional state of the woman? Is she normally a very stable person, or does she have high and low phases? Since becoming pregnant, what is her emotional state? Much here will depend on the conditions in which she became pregnant. Presumably in most abortion cases, there was no intention to become pregnant. It was an accident or a crime. Perhaps the contraceptive failed, or there was no attempt to stop pregnancy. This might have been due to ignorance, alcohol or drugs, carelessness, or sheer optimism. 'We won't get caught out.' It might have been due to assault. It is possible for assault to take place within a marriage as well as outside it. Was there assault or rape involved? Was the woman simply the victim or did she play some part in causing the situation? The emotional state of the woman will vary both according to the circumstances which led to pregnancy and also to the pressures which are leading to the possibility of abortion. Is this a desire on her part? Has she been (or is she being) pressurized by father, parents, family or friends? Is there economic pressure involved?

The very fact that she is pregnant may be upsetting her emotional state. Some would argue that being pregnant is to be in a highly charged emotional condition. How is she coping with the fact of being pregnant emotionally? This, of course, leads to consideration of how she will cope at the emotional level either with termination of pregnancy or with continuance of pregnancy. Is she likely to be affected by guilt and depression? There is evidence of post-abortive trauma in many cases of termination of pregnancy. Will continuing with the pregnancy lead to depression, and perhaps even to mental breakdown? Is the woman able to sustain the emotional strain of pregnancy, birth, and bringing up (or giving up) a young baby? The answers to these questions depend not only on the woman's emotional state, but her physical well-being as well as the family and economic situation at home.

(ii) Physical health

Is the mother-to-be well? Is she physically fit and healthy? Has she suffered physical harm in being pregnant, through assault or rape? Is her general condition one of fitness and good health? Has being pregnant affected her physical health and are there changes to her well-being if she remains pregnant? Likewise, it is important to consider whether she is able to stand the strain of an operation and the physical stress of an anaesthetic, as well as any physical discomfort which may arise because of termination. Will she remain healthy, if she continues the pregnancy? Will an abortion affect her physical ability to have more children? This last possibility is extremely unlikely, yet may be a real concern to women who are in the situation of seeking abortion. Has she the physical strength and fitness necessary to fulfil the term of pregnancy, give birth, and begin to nurture and look after a young baby?

(c)   THE MOTHER'S SITUATION

It is a moot point whether it is proper to talk of 'mother' rather than simply woman or 'expectant mother'. Yet it is crucial to know the woman's situation. We have already asked questions to discover the circumstances that led both to pregnancy and to the request for termination or its possibility being considered. These factors need to be set in the context of home, work, relationships, her reflection on the areas of life, and her own moral and religious beliefs. What is the home situation? Is she married, single or separated? Does she live with her husband? Are her parents in the home or nearby? Is there a family involved, both in the sense of a family of her own (born, adopted or acquired in marriage) and a family of brothers, sisters and other relations? What is the quality of relationships? Is the woman happy and secure? Is this happiness and security threatened by a child or another child? Will termination cause problems with family? Will a new baby create problems in the home, with the husband, the children (if any), or any others who are there? Obviously the quality of relationships and the ability of these relationships to withstand the pressure of a decision to terminate or a decision to continue the pregnancy, are major factors in understanding the woman herself and advising her, if we are in that position.

It also makes a difference to our consideration, if the woman is working. How does she see this work? Is it a necessity, financially or personally satisfying, or a hobby? Will a baby affect this? Will she be able to return to work? Will her career prospects be harmed? What is the attitude of her employers and workmates? What will their reaction be whichever solution is adopted? Obviously in these areas of relationships and the situation, we are concerned with two main things. What the actual situation is and how the woman perceives her own situation. These may not be the same. A pregnant woman, like all of us, may have a different perception of reality from the reality itself. Part of how she perceives herself and her situation will be a reflection of her own moral and religious beliefs. We shall return to these themes below in discussion of (h) and (k), but it is worth noting that the woman will have some moral views and possibly religious beliefs as well. She may believe that killing in any form is wrong or that people should be free to choose whatever they wish to do regardless. She may believe in a God to whom she is answerable and responsible, or that childbirth is the means of salvation. Whatever her beliefs are in the moral and religious realms, it is important that we discover these beliefs and the significance they hold for the woman.

(i) Family pressure

The mother's health and situation are partly a reflection on the support or otherwise she is experiencing from her family. This includes both her husband and children, as well as parents and relatives. Again there may be a difference between what is actually the case and what the woman feels is the case. Likewise, others may say one thing; yet their behaviour and attitude show that they mean something quite different. What kind of pressure is there from the other children and husband? Is it enough that they would like another brother or sister? Do they know of the pregnancy? How did they react and what is the likely long-term reaction to a new arrival? Will this affect the family balances in both the economic and psychological senses? Is the father/husband supportive of the woman? Will he support regardless of the decision? Has he a particular preference?

What are the feelings of the woman's parents and relations? In the case of a single woman, this is the greatest area of pressure. Those who are often anti-abortion in general terms will plead strongly for an abortion for their daughter. Married women too come under pressure from parents and relatives. This may be both to have or to abort the child. This kind of pressure may be applied in subtle ways, yet it is very real and affects the woman and her decision. Particularly important is the extent to which such pressure has forced the woman to suggest abortion, and the extent to which it is a genuine expression of her own will and desires.

(ii) Consequences and choice

These categories must be dealt with in their own rights (see (v) and (w) below), but it is proper to recognize that the consequences of abortion or continuing the pregnancy to term are very great for the woman. Her life for the next few months at least and probably for many years to come will be radically affected by the decision taken in this situation. She will either move from expectant motherhood to the reality of mothering, or else undergo an abortion and lose the foetus. Her relationships with the father, her own children, parents, relatives and friends could be altered by the choices made, as well as her career, future relationships, economic and personal well-being. She is all too aware that the consequences of the decision will not simply affect her, but have far-reaching effects on many others.

It is yet to be discussed who ought to make the decision to abort or to prolong the pregnancy. For some it is the absolute right of the woman herself to make the choice. We shall see the arguments supporting the right of others to make that choice, but such a view must deal with the woman's own choice. The critics of the woman's right to choose rest their case on the fitness of the woman to make the choice. This is not only a difficulty, when brutality is involved, but the very state of being pregnant and having the option of an abortion may themselves hinder the woman's ability and capacity to make a rational choice, which will satisfy her in the long term. It is argued that pregnant women are notoriously contrary in their feelings and desires. To fasten on a decision of one moment may be to ignore the possibility of a change of heart at the next. However, the question then becomes an extremely tendentious one, for, if the woman is not to choose, who will choose instead?

(d) THE FOETUS

When we come to consider the foetus, its condition, status and rights, we are immediately confronted with the problem of definitions. It is important to define life and what it means to be a person. This will lead to some consideration of the foetus in relation to law, public opinion, moral and religious values and beliefs, and finally to consider the consequences for the foetus of a decision to go to term or to terminate the pregnancy.

(i)   The condition of the foetus

Our concern, and that of the medical staff, is to know the physical condition of the foetus. Is the baby normal or deformed? What is the degree of deformity? How certain is the diagnosis and how reliable the testing? Some feel that abortion is more a possibility in the circumstances of defective life. They deny that abnormal, deformed existence is human life. To be born abnormal, imbecilic, hydrocephalic, or a congenital syphilitic is to have no real prospect of human existence. Such a life of suffering is no life at all. Others would disagree most strongly. No matter the condition of the foetus, this is the realm of human life. If there are medical problems for the foetus, we must do all we can, not only to preserve life, but to bring about the highest quality of life which is possible for that foetus. If there is no prospect of life whatsoever, nature itself will intervene by spontaneous abortion. This natural argument will be considered under the heading of 'natural law' below.

(ii)   The definition of life (r)

The problem of the definition of life is not simply how to give a biological account. It is rather how to define the moment when human life begins. This is more difficult than it seems and there are a number of conflicting theories. Some stress that life begins at the moment of *fertilization* when the male sperm fertilizes the female ovum or egg. Others pick the moment of *implantation* when the fertilized egg fastens itself to the wall of the womb. Expectant mothers tend to claim that life begins when first they feel the baby move inside them—the moment of *quickening*. Others suggest that *viability* of life is the crucial moment. This is the moment when the foetus is able to survive outside the mother's womb, though this survival may be only possible in an incubator in a special care unit for premature babies. This viability factor is an ever-decreasing figure, for it is not unknown nowadays for babies of only 21–22 weeks to survive. At one time, twenty-eight weeks seemed the general viability figure. Hence the terms of the Abortion Act.

That viability figure is now much lower and may continue to fall. Others argue that human life only begins properly when *birth* takes place. Life begins at birth. The pedantic may argue that human life proper is only present when we are fully independent of others for our physical survival. On this theory it is likely that some of us will never be fully human.

Some have tried a different style of approach to the definition of life by drawing a distinction between actual and potential human life. They would argue that the difference between a pregnant woman and a foetus is that one is an actual human being while the other is only potentially a human being. The science of genetics is used to bolster this view. From the moment of fertilization the foetus is programmed by genetic material, so that he (or she) will—if they grow to full maturity—become a particular height, shape, colour, and personality. Others have belittled the search for a 'magic moment' when life begins. Simply because we are unable to specify the exact moment, does not mean that there is no such moment, nor that life is not truly present.

(iii) The definition of a person (s)

Closely allied to the debate over the beginnings of life, is the question of what defines a person. Is the foetus a person? To answer this question, one must have some notion of what constitutes personhood. Traditionally, that has been seen as a question of 'having a soul'. If one believes in the soul, then one is left with the prior problem of when the soul enters the body and all the answers to the previous question of when life begins have been offered as responses to the timing of 'ensoulment'. In this materialistically-minded age, the notion of a soul and a soul–body relationship are not very popular. Yet people still recognize personhood and seek to offer some definition of its nature. For some, to be a person is to be capable of rational thought. Other definitions stress responsibility and answerability, or the capacity to form and maintain human relationships. This creates difficulty for those who are insane, children, who have yet to come to the fullness of human behaviour, and, of course, for the foetus. Usually personhood is still assigned to the insane and children on the grounds of what they have been or what they will or may become.

It is in the latter category that the foetus may belong as yet to become fully a person.

Ordinary people have little sympathy with philosophical arguments over metaphysical questions, for example, what is something in and of itself? They know what a person is, but find the category of the foetus in the womb a real difficulty. The mother and father may have a nickname for the foetus. He or she is a real person to them especially from the moment of quickening when life can be seen and felt. Retrospectively, people do refer to the foetus in terms of the person they now know. We all know the situation of the small child asking where he or she was at a particular time before birth. We talk about the time when 'John was on the way'. This implies some kind of person and personality, yet not a fully-fledged one. It is a similar difficulty to that of the definition of life.

(iv)   The foetus in law

In recent law cases, there have been claims made on behalf of the foetus, and it has been recognized that the foetus has some rights in this respect. Damages for injuries incurred before birth in road accidents have been awarded to children, who continue to suffer because of their experiences. It is also possible that one might sue successfully for damages in the case where a foetus is lost as a result of an accident. In Old Testament times there was a fine involved for the loss of a foetus if a man injured a woman so that she aborted. The foetus had a value and worth, even if this worth was less than that of a mature person. It is clear that the foetus has rights in law, but these rights are limited. The foetus may inherit and his or her well-being is safeguarded to the extent that injuries received *in utero* may be compensated for in later life. No claims, however, may be made against the foetus for harm it might do to the mother; thus the case is more like that of minors, which is no great surprise.

(v)   The foetus and public opinion

Few people, except the activists or those who are involved with pregnancy, seem to give much thought to the status of the foetus. The demand for abortion and the relative ease with which it is available, suggests that public opinion has little regard for the foetus. The recent Italian referendum on abortion reveals that the right of the woman is overwhelming in contrast to the right of the foetus. Yet there are two specific areas of public opinion which contrast with this. The first is the attitude of the anti-abortion lobby, e.g. the Society for the Protection of the Unborn Child (SPUC) and 'Life'. Their 'high' view of the rights and status of the foetus and the value of his or her life leads them to active attempts to change and modify the law and public opinion. Literature and publicity are geared to an appeal to public opinion and morality in an attempt to put pressure on the legislators to amend the abortion laws.

It is also the case that among the medical and nursing practitioners in obstetrics and the mother and father of the foetus, there is a stronger awareness of the foetus. This reveals itself in the way of referring to the foetus, the language and even 'pet' names given to the being in the womb. This is not to be confused with the retrospective references we all fall into, when we talk of the time when 'Mary was on the way'. For some 'Mary' was 'Mary' from an early time in the pregnancy. For others, it is simply a way of dating other events in relation to present existents, rather than a solid basis for reflection on the ontological status of the foetus.

(vi) The foetus and moral and religious values and beliefs (h, k)

In dealing with the definitions of life and personhood, we have been moving into the moral and religious realms. These definitions are not solely legal concerns, though they may be vital within the jurisdiction of the law courts and our legal systems. What we believe a person to be and our views on the nature of life are fundamental parts of our moral and religious values and beliefs. Every system of morality carries with it some notion of the sanctity of life and the limits of taking life. Life is to be preserved under specified conditions. It is easy to be misled here by different cultural practices. We imagine that moralities vary as much as those cultural practices. The Spartans put male babies on exposed hillsides soon after birth. Modern man ensures that babies are safely enclosed in hospitals, in incubators, in totally secure settings. This seems to suggest that life is more precious today than it was long ago. There may well be ways we cling to life today, which do suggest that it has an overwhelming importance for us, but life mattered to Spartan mothers, fathers and society a great deal. As a small city-state, survival was crucial. That meant strong armies, which in turn required a steady supply of able young men. The first step towards producing a generation of hardy soldiers was exposure. The weak did not survive, while the young survivors were nurtured to full development with the best that Sparta could provide. Life mattered, though this life was only healthy life. The moral framework in our two examples here influences the behaviour towards the foetus. Thus it is vital to clarify the underlying moral values of those involved in the possible abortion situation. We shall examine below the moral views of the mother, father, medical and nursing staff, the law and of the general public (h). What is vital is the knowledge that people have moral values concerning the nature of life and what constitutes a person. These moral values find expression not only in the language we all use, but in our personal behaviour and social and legal attitudes.

If this is true with reference to moral values, it is also true in relation to religious beliefs (k). For many, their morality has a direct relation with their religious orientation. For them morality is grounded in their religion. It is accordingly vital to clarify what religious beliefs are at work among those concerned with the possibility of an abortion. The nature and intensity of these beliefs is important and the degree to which they may be overridden is also important. Many Jehovah's Witnesses refuse to permit blood transfusions on religious grounds. In the case of their children, some local authorities in England have taken the legal step of removing the child from parental care into local authority custody. The local authority has then given permission for transfusion to the child. Obviously, it is the judgement of the courts and local authority officers that preservation of life is more important than permitting religious beliefs to specify the treatment of a minor. This is not to suggest that religious beliefs have no place in tricky medical situations, but to clarify that the state, the medical profession and the law may seek to limit the influence of such religious beliefs, if these appear to conflict with generally accepted moral standards.

This tension and limiting may work in a variety of ways. For a long time there was considerable pressure for a change in the abortion laws of this country, but the medical profession in particular played a cautious delaying role. Traditionally the medical profession tends to be conservative and recent attempts to alter the Abortion Act have failed to gain the support of the medical world. There remains a high level of ethical behaviour expected and indeed required by the medical profession, which seeks to police its own members and to ensure high ethical standards.

(vii) Consequences for the foetus (v)

While we shall show that the consequence of any decision to terminate or to facilitate the completion of a pregnancy are far-reaching (v), it is self-evident that the consequences are most serious for the foetus. If there is a decision to terminate, the foetus will die. Some would express this much more forcibly. The foetus will be killed or murdered. Unasked, unknowing, the life of the foetus would come to an end, though many argue that some techniques of abortion do cause severe pain and suffering to the foetus. Life will end, and the significance of that fact weighs heavily in the moral and religious dimensions and attitudes to abortion.

In contrast, the decision to allow the pregnancy to go to its full term means that the foetus will be born, all being well. Thus a new life will enter the world and will affect and be affected by many people. Time, effort and a series of developing relationships enable the foetus to fulfil the potential of full human life. For the handicapped child this is a bone of contention in the abortion debate. There is no doubt that medical science is able to predict with increasing accuracy the likely physical and mental state of the foetus and the possibility and degree of handicap the foetus will have. At the same time, we know the quality of life and of care that handicapped people experience. Some argue that this knowledge is very limited, for who can enter into the experience of those whose lives are so fundamentally different from our own. This does not necessarily mean that there is contentment or happiness with the quality of life experienced. Ignorance of another's experience cannot be positively construed as offering satisfaction, though such ignorance does suggest the need for caution in making sweeping judgements as to the handicapped person's perception (or lack of perception) of his (her) state. It is also unclear to us how medical science will progress with new drugs and techniques for the treatment of handicapped people. Again this unknown will not serve in itself as an excuse for abortion or for refusal to abort. There needs to be some additional moral or clinical factor to sway the argument in one direction or the other.

Even if we were totally clear as to the degree and experience of handicap, it is less clear what value we can place on the quality of life, either on behalf of the handicapped person himself (herself) or in relation to our own criteria of the value of life. Some feel that if there is a high degree of handicap and that this will seriously impair the quality of life enjoyed by the foetus, when born, then termination should be automatic or at the very least available to the parents. This immediately brings in the consequences of abortion or non-abortion for others. It is argued that it is unreasonable to expect parents to cope with an extremely severely handicapped child. Indeed, some would doubt the wisdom of expecting society through its medical and nursing resources to cope with extreme handicap. It is crucial to separate the two strands in the pro-abortion case built on consequences. The first unacceptable consequence is the quality of life of the handicapped person. The second unacceptable consequence is the pain, pressure and demands to be endured by parents and society, if the pregnancy is not terminated.

The counter argument tends to proceed by casting doubt on our ability to predict either set of consequences with any accuracy. If we do not know, we cannot terminate. However, we have seen that doubt and ignorance themselves are insufficient as moral grounds for refusing an abortion. The truth of the moral matter is that the refusal to countenance abortion rests on the belief that no matter the consequences, it is wrong to take life and to deprive any handicapped person of any quality of life, no matter what that may be and what such life will entail for those who must care for the handicapped person. On this view, life itself is inherently precious and to be preserved at all costs. Obviously this states the extreme, though it is the ground behind much unease concerning abortion on the grounds of handicap.

There is one further consequence to be noted and that is the famous wedge argument. If we allow a handicapped foetus to be killed today, then tomorrow it may be healthy babies, children and adults, whose lives are 'unacceptable' to the majority of society. We shall examine this wedge argument below (v), but it is interesting to note the phrase, 'it may be', for that doubt is the weakness in the presentation of such a position. Such doubt is equally applicable to the pro- and anti-abortion arguments based on the likely effects of illegitimacy. When an unmarried mother asks for an abortion, the consequences of being born illegitimate are avoided. This is the pro-abortion line, but we cannot tell whether the stigma of illegitimacy will destroy the child or cause him (her) to succeed against all opposition and abuse. Not knowing means that we cannot use either possible set of consequences as grounds for a decision to allow or reject an abortion.

The consequences, however, for the foetus from a decision to abort or to refuse an abortion are the most total imaginable. It is literally a matter of life and death for the foetus and that fact weighs heavily with all who are called on to make any decision concerning abortions. It should be so, for the taking of life is at the very limit of our human relationships in society and is final. Care must be exercised in making such momentous decisions.

(e) THE ISSUE OF RIGHTS

We have previously examined the main concerns about rights which centre on the rights of the woman and of the foetus—(a)(i), (ii), (d)(iv). We saw that the case for women's rights rested on the fact that women carry the foetus and the claim that it is a parasite on the woman. A woman should be free to do with her own body whatever she wishes. Particularly important are the situations where the woman's rights have been infringed. Rape, incest and forced sex within marriage are conditions where abortion should be freely available. More contentious is the claim that a woman has an absolute right to full social, psychological and physical health. If a pregnancy threatens this health, it ought to be terminated.

In sharp contrast stand the rights of the foetus to life itself. Since the foetus is unable to defend and claim his (her) own rights, society and the law must be extremely concerned to safeguard the rights of the foetus. The difficulty is that abortion situations are rarely a clear-cut choice between the rights of the woman and those of the foetus. There are the rights of many others to be considered. The father of the child has rights. He bears a share in responsibility for the conception and is entitled to some say in any decision affecting the life of the foetus. Recent legal decisions have tended to subsume such rights under the rights of the mother of the foetus. Thus a husband cannot force his wife to continue a pregnancy if she wishes to have an abortion and that abortion falls within the permitted cases. Yet the father ought to be consulted and to accept his responsibility for the foetus.

One main difficulty in the demand for abortion in the safety and security of hospital is that this involves others. Doctors and nurses have a vital role to play and many are happy so to do. There are, however, those who, on moral and religious grounds, refuse to play any part in abortions. Once abortions become permissible in law, the position of such doctors and nurses becomes a major concern. The law itself framed a 'conscience clause', which allowed conscientious objectors the right to refuse to take part in abortions. They were to suffer no harm to their careers on the grounds of their decision. In theory, this remains true, but many feel the pressure on junior staff to be involved in abortions is very great. In busy gynaecological wards, where all the staff are under pressure, the refusal to participate in certain procedures will inevitably arouse hostility. This may affect the future prospects of the objector and his (her) personal relationships with other staff.

Society too has some rights in these matters. By having abortion laws, which reflect a change in public opinion, society is expressing its acquiescence in the abortion of the foetus under certain specified conditions. That such conditions are specified shows that action outside these conditions infringes on society's rights and society through the law will act to punish such infringement.

All the various rights mentioned here are subject to two levels of check. The first check arises from the possible conflict of rights between interested parties; thus there must be some hierarchy of rights in difficult cases. Morality, religion and the law are looked to as the ground of such an hierarchy. The second check lies in the awareness that claims to rights are accompanied by the under-taking of obligations. One person's rights are another person's obligations. This interaction of rights and responsibilities means that any exercise of a right occurs in the context where obligations and responsibilities are fulfilled. There must, therefore, be sufficient grounds for such fulfilment to take place, and this inevitably leads back to the morality and legality of any decision concerning an abortion.

(f) THE LAW

Properly to understand the present abortion laws in Britain, we need to sketch in the situation before. Abortions, it seems, have always happened throughout history. Such abortions were illegal. Thus abortion was driven underground. The main argument in favour of legal abortion traditionally rested on the necessity of solving the problem of back-street abortions. Many women in desperation at being pregnant would seek help from unqualified people, who performed their work in unsterile conditions and often lacked genuine medical or nursing knowledge and skill. Gin, knitting needles, hot baths, emetic powders, and risky operations produced a stream of fatalities, sterility and many casualties. Some doctors and nurses, appalled at the suffering, risked their professional reputations to serve those who required an abortion. If caught, this led to criminal prosecution, usually under the Offences Against Persons Act of 1861 or the Infant Life (Preservation) Act of 1929. Abortion was not totally banned. If the mother's life was at risk, the medical staff were safeguarded under law in performing an abortion.

Given the abuses of the back-street abortionists, the high rate of those seeking abortions, the risks to the medical profession, and the general change in the moral and social climate of opinion on the issue of abortion, it was possible for the Abortion Act of 1967 to become law. Under the terms of the law, termination of pregnancy is permitted if the risk to the mother's health and life is greater than the risk of terminating, if the foetus is severely abnormal, and if the whole environment of the mother, both social and psychological, is such as to indicate that an abortion should be performed. There are three further conditions set on the grounds for abortion. The first is that the termination should occur before the twenty-eighth week of pregnancy. The second that two doctors should give permission for the termination. The third is the presence of the so-called conscience clause, allowing doctors and nurses freedom to refuse to participate in abortive procedures.

The pro- and anti-abortion camps are both agreed that this law ought to be changed. Of course, they disagree fundamentally about the direction of such changes. The pro-abortionist argues for more flexible, open abortion laws, while the anti-abortionist argues for more restrictive laws. There are certain problems and abuses of the law which concern all those involved in the application of the law. There has been financial abuse by private clinics who have charged exorbitant rates and have attracted a world-wide clientele for their abortion services. This example of the profit motive has led many to suggest that only National Health Service hospitals should be used. Others have been concerned that the twenty-eight week limit is out of step with modern improvements in neo-natal care. Some have argued for the lowering of the limit to twenty-four or twenty weeks, bringing that limit nearer to the time of viability of the foetus. Others have argued that there should be no such time limit whatsoever and abortions should be available at any stage of pregnancy.

There has been widespread concern at the way the law has been interpreted particularly with reference to the social and psychological grounds for abortion. Some feel that far too liberal and easy interpreting of these conditions has virtually created a situation of abortion on demand. The reasons for abortion are often trivial; yet abortions are not difficult to procure. Others feel that a major problem is the lack of time for proper counselling for the woman. With medical and nursing staff under the pressure of busy clinics, it is little wonder that there may not be sufficient time to discuss the woman's request for abortion. The alternatives may not be fully considered and the woman may not be given sufficient support to cope with her decision, whatever that may be.

The example of other countries is often used by both sides in the abortion debate, but this may not be helpful, for the examples and situations are never exactly the same and the counter-claims may seem to cancel each other out. There are many activists from both sides engaged in seeking to influence parliamentarians and public opinion. Both sides have vigorous press and advertising campaigns, as well as public meetings. This shows clearly that the law is seen as a reflection of the mood and morality of the country as a whole. If that mood can be changed, then the law may be affected. Here again the role of morality and religious values is vital. Because people perceive abortion in a particular way, they are prepared to work very hard to change the present situation to conform to their ideal. The democratic processes of the West allow such debate, but also ensure that the majority view, whether of the Houses of Parliament or of public opinion, will win the day. It is that majority opinion which must be captured if the law is to be changed.

(g) THE FATHER

It is all too easy for the role of the father to be ignored in the abortion issue. Yet his part in the circumstances may be vital. He may be a rapist, under-age and have very strong anti-abortion views. He shares responsibility for the life of the foetus, and ought to play a part in any final decision. More than likely he will be directly affected by the pregnancy and by the decision to continue or terminate that pregnancy. If there is termination, his relationship with the mother will be vital. If the pregnancy continues, especially if there is any possibility of handicap, he will have a key role to play in the home. His own physical and psychological state is important. His scale of moral and religious values and beliefs may radically affect the final decision taken. He has some rights in that situation, though, as we have seen, there are limits to those rights. He will be a key figure in the support of the mother in whatever decision is made.

(h) MORAL VALUES

As is already clear, the abortion issue is hotly debated by differing moral viewpoints. For the Christian making moral decisions, it is the drawing up of the first important principles below, which is the important step. But such decisions must be taken in awareness of the alternative moral viewpoints. The issues on which moral divergence occurs are the value of life, the nature of a person, and the proper expressions of sexuality. For the anti-abortionist, of whom the Roman Catholic position is typical, life is sacred and to be preserved at all costs without exception, the foetus is a person from the earliest moments of life. These views often are accompanied by a strict attitude towards sexual intercourse, holding that this is proper only within the marriage relationship and ought to be directed towards procreation. The opposite extreme of the pro-abortion case may be typified by the supporter of women's liberation. This view would argue that the foetus is in no way a proper person and has no significance in comparison with the rights of the mother. Life in the foetal form is not sacred and need not be preserved, especially if there is some negative cost to the woman carrying the foetus. Sexuality and sexual expression are interpreted as freely available for women on a pleasure basis and need not have any procreative aspect, unless this is the specific aim of the woman.

There are various middle positions, which try to argue both that life has great moral significance, but also that the circumstances of the pregnancy and the likely consequences may call for responses of compassion. In such situations termination of pregnancy must be permitted. These situations should be exceptional and such exceptions ought not to be the norm. In some ways this argument holds that life matters, the foetus is a potential rather than an actual person, and thus abortion may be the lesser of two evils. Even with a 'high' doctrine of sexuality, such a middle course would recognize the frailty and fallibility of human beings and permit abortion in cases where abuse of sexual expression has occurred, or where the consequences of such sexual activity would be harmful to those concerned.

It is appropriate here to note that the hard line position need not be totally rigid in refusing abortions. There is a moral argument called the Law of Double Effect. It argues that I am responsible for the intended results of my action rather than any consequences which may happen to follow from my action, as long as those consequences were not my intention. Thus a doctor may operate on a pregnant woman. His intention is to save the woman's life. He has no wish to harm the foetus. However, as a result of his action, the unintended consequence of foetal death may follow. The doctor is not strictly responsible for such consequences, for if he could have saved the mother's life in some other way, he would have done so. Unfortunately, it is extremely difficult to have certainty in the realm of intentions. Usually we depend on what others tell us they intend to do and on the fact that they try to do it. Thus there are no clearly objective tests to enable us to be sure of another's intentions.

Different moral positions lead to different moral and practical conclusions. There is little doubt that morality is important in the abortion issue. Indeed some would argue that the real moral issue is not abortion itself, but the conditions that lead to the necessity for abortions and the requests for them. In a sense, every abortion is a confession of failure, whether individual or social. It requires moral education in the realm of sexuality, proper personal relationships, and responsibility in our behaviour. Such moral issues are as fundamental as those concerning the value of life and the nature of personhood. How we deal with alternative moral views will be further explored, when we examine other people's viewpoints (OPV).

Given that morality is crucial in the abortion issue, it is necessary to be clear. What different moral viewpoints are held by those affected by the situation? Thus we need to explore the moral values of the mother, father, medical and nursing staff, the law and public opinion. This will clarify the ground, though it will not, in itself, enable us to decide an order of priority between different values.

(i) FAMILY PRESSURES

For both the single and married woman contemplating an abortion, there may be considerable pressure from parents and relatives. They may have very strong moral and religious views, and as strong views concerning the well-being and future of the woman herself. It is not uncommon for those who are in theory most fiercely opposed to abortion, to demand most vehemently an abortion for their own daughter, if the circumstances are difficult. This pressure is as subtle or as blatant as every form of human relationship. Our capacity to cajole, persuade or force each other to do things seems almost unlimited. The pregnant woman may be the butt of such manifold pressures and this will add to the distress and difficulty of arriving at a conclusion. This is particularly the case, if she feels the decision should be genuinely her own.

In similar fashion, the father of the child and, in the case of a married couple, any family on the scene may put pressure on the woman. Again, this may not be so much a stated, verbal pressure, but the woman's own concern for their welfare or a change in their behaviour. The likely consequences for a family of another child, especially if this is an unwanted, unplanned event, may seem disastrous. We must say 'may seem', for it is extremely difficult to foresee exactly what the results will actually be. The optimist will stress the human capacity to cope and overcome, regardless of difficulty. The pessimist will make gloomy remarks about collapse, insanity and disaster. What is clear is that at a point where the woman is vulnerable, she may be subject to tremendous pressures, which may indeed conflict. The support she is offered, if any, may be conditional on reaching the appropriate conclusion. That is to agree with the family view. Unmarried mothers have found this kind of pressure extremely difficult, especially if they wish to have their child. Various organizations exist to try to help in these circumstances, but it is hard, particularly for the under-age mother.

(j) PUBLIC OPINION

While it is difficult to be exact as to the state of public opinion on any issue (see fluctuations in opinion polls), it is clear that there has been a dramatic shift in the attitudes towards abortion. From being unmentionable in polite society and a criminal matter, it has become a normal part of many lives. The National Abortion Campaign record that 'on current trends, at least one in four of all women in Britain will have at least one abortion in her lifetime'. (January 1980, Press release, NAC) There is no doubt that the rate of abortions has increased since 1967 and that many foetuses have died, who would have survived, if there had been no change in the law.

In the search for public opinion on the issue, it is difficult to know where to begin and to end. The pressure groups reveal both support from public opinion and the obvious necessity to convince the unconvinced. There would be no press releases or public campaigning, if public opinion was solidly of one mind. Looking to the law and parliament may not help give a conclusive picture of public opinion, for the 'mother of parliaments' is notoriously out of step with public feeling on many issues, for example, hanging or the EEC, so the same may be true of abortion. In addition, parliamentarians are themselves divided as to the direction and degree of change necessary in the abortion laws. It is difficult to see here whether parliament in legal changes follows the line of public opinion or creates that public opinion. This makes the work of the pressure groups all the more significant.

The same is true of the media. Obviously there is a strong sense in which the media create public views and fuel particular causes. Some would argue that this is simply a case of giving people what they want to hear and believe. Others would take a more sinister view of press, radio and television activities. What adds to the confusion is local and regional variation. Traditionally the Scots and the Irish are more conscientious in moral matters than the English and the law (e.g. on homosexuality) has tended to reflect that conservatism.

Public opinion may be very significant for the woman, her family and friends, and for the medical and nursing staff, as they debate the possibility of an abortion. That significance may lead to a calm acquiescence or a grim determination to swim against the tide. Yet it is vital that those involved be aware of the ground swell of public opinion and the likely consequence of action which does not agree with the popular line.

(k) RELIGIOUS BELIEFS (FIP)

The details of the main Christian views on abortion will be examined under the heading of First Important Principles. The fact that people do have religious beliefs and values which affect their attitudes towards abortion is the important point. Religious beliefs about the sanctity of life, the nature of personhood, the proper expressions of sexuality, compassion, mercy and forgiveness, all have a vital role in the abortion debate. It is important to clarify the content of the woman's own beliefs, those of the father, and of the medical and nursing staff. For the Christian involved in discussion of the abortion issue, whether in theory or in a pastoral context, it is vital that he (she) examines the content of his (her) own religious beliefs. This means what the Church teaches, what the Scripture has to say, and to discern the actual practice of Christians in relation to abortion. Such a list suggests that there may well be a gap between theory and practice. The same may be true on the part of those involved in the situation of an abortion.

This gap creates problems for those involved in counselling. Are we to demand consistency from people? Is that consistency to conform to our moral and religious standards or to their own? Guilt and distress often follow the breaking of religious rules and the doing of what is perceived as wrong. How should this guilt be relieved, if indeed it ought to be? This raises questions about the degree of directiveness appropriate in counselling (u) (p. 120), and the proper degree of involvement. If the Church is proclaiming a rigid anti-abortion line, it is vital that the Church then takes responsibility for the consequences of that decision in terms of care for the mother and the child, both in the short and long term. Any public proclamation of standards requires consistency in the living of those standards and in coping with the consequences of such standards.

However, even if we may be clear as Christians what our standards actually are, we may be confronted by the force of circumstances affecting our decision. The mother may not feel as we do. She may decide differently. This creates problems all along the line. The general practitioner, who refuses to have any dealings with abortions, may have a patient who does not share his religious outlook. To what extent may the doctor enforce his

111

morality on the patient and make it difficult for the patient to gain access to an abortion? On the other hand, the regular practitioner of abortion, confronted with a confused, deeply religious, pregnant woman, may advise an abortion, without any awareness of her unease or the possible consequences of her action.

While it seems perfectly proper to campaign and advocate changes in law and public opinion, we are less easy in forcing our morality on those who are vulnerable. At the same time, if our religious beliefs are true, then we have a responsibility to proclaim these religious standards and to advocate them forcefully. Yet, in the end, we must allow people the freedom to reject our views. Where this line of debate runs into problems is where the rejection of particular religious and moral views causes unacceptable harm to others and, indeed, to the person themselves. Thus we return to the issues of the sanctity of life, the nature of a person, and the freedom of individuals to make their own choices.

(I) SEXUAL EXPRESSION

The conditions under which the pregnancy occurred are significant in the approach to abortion. It may have been a situation of rape, incest, or under-age sexual intercourse. As the law stands, these would normally themselves be sufficient grounds for an abortion, if requested. The anti-abortionist is uneasy that such *carte blanche* exists without careful exploration of the maternal and feminine instincts which may be at work and being fulfilled, even in those unlikely circumstances. Alternatives ought to be put, not least the possibility of adoption of the child and direct support of mother and child if the mother so wishes.

The situation with the unmarried mother is more difficult. Some feel that abortion is an easy way to avoid the consequences of one's actions, and ought to be difficult to obtain. Behind this is considerable unease as to the morality of sexual relationships outside of marriage. Abortion, it is claimed, is being used as a late form of contraception. The same may be true of the married woman who finds herself pregnant and unable to cope with the prospect of a child given her circumstances and life at present. This is where attention turns to the limiting conditions within the abortion laws, especially the social and psychological grounds.

For some, the way and circumstances of conception are irrelevant to the situation now. There is a foetus to be considered. In contrast, the woman's own freedom may be at risk. Thus, even if the sexual circumstances are ignored, no agreement will necessarily be reached as to the propriety of abortion. Nevertheless, for many the sexual circumstances are vital, for they may be themselves criminal. The innocent should not be required to suffer in such circumstances, but that still leaves the issue of the innocent foetus. Only the most extreme would argue that the foetus is an irrelevance in abortion decisions. Trivial grounds for abortion are unacceptable to most people and this is likely to remain so in a culture where such store is set by the having and bringing up of children.

(m) ECONOMICS

Any trip down the High Street of any town will soon reveal the economic dimension to the having, clothing and feeding of a child. The economic factors in the abortion situation are, however, more complex than the actual cost of having the baby and whether this cost can be afforded. Government allowances and the National Health Service mean that maternity is not nearly so expensive in Britain as in many other countries. The economic issues tend to centre much more on the mother. She may already be a working woman. To continue with the pregnancy means not only an interruption of her career and wage-earning, but perhaps a more permanent interruption. Recent legislation has tried to preserve jobs in maternity cases, but there are many ways round laws and many pressures at a time of high unemployment. If the pregnancy continues the long-term economic situation of the woman and of her husband and family may be adversely affected. This may be a significant factor in what may be already difficult economic circumstances. The woman may be the sole or major wage-earner. Even where her income is a genuinely second income, that may have become a necessity for the survival or for the life-style the family have adopted.

Closely tied with the financial aspects are the career prospects. With high unemployment and the history of discrimination in employment against women, there is a genuine fear that an interruption of a career may be fatal or at least handicapping in the long term to promotion prospects. These effects on the woman may likewise be mirrored to a lesser extent in the father's situation. The extra drain on finances may seem too great to be contemplated.

Part of the dilemma in contemplating the abortion issue at anything more than the personal level is that it opens up a Pandora's box of social and international problems. Given economic recession world-wide and the British government's policy of financial cutbacks, the cost of abortion services and of maternity units must come under scrutiny. If the National Health Service is to be cut, should these cuts come in the abortion services or in the maternity and fertility services? Is it advisable to spend large sums on resources and staffing in either the termination or the close support of pregnancies? On a more global scale, the problems of over-population and of food shortages raise questions not only about contraception, but also of the use of abortion as a palliative to relieve these problems. Singapore in particular has embarked on a programme of population control in which abortion plays a significant part. The difficulty is that it is hard to legislate for world-wide practice making proper allowances for the different circumstances of Calcutta and Coventry. Whether it is proper to use abortion techniques in this way is open to debate, but it is clear that the economic factors, both personal and national, are important.

(n) PREJUDICE AND EMOTION

Abortion is an emotive issue. It arouses strong feelings on all sides. Such strength of feeling makes debate and rational argument difficult, for when we feel strongly on an issue we tend not to listen and to overstate our case. Of course, the abortion issue lends itself to emotive treatment for it concerns the growth and development of a child, the consequences of intimate sexual expression, and the very basic feelings of femininity and motherhood. The treatment of the issues involved may very easily become propaganda and be designed to arouse emotions. Even the language we use to describe the abortion is feeling-laden. An abortion may be either an 'evacuation of the uterus' or 'scraping the baby out'. It may be a 'simple surgical procedure' or 'murder'.

If feelings run high among those discussing abortion, they are even more keenly felt among those at the sharp point of the problem. The woman is naturally subject to a welter of different emotions and responses, as a woman to being pregnant, considering an abortion, and subject to medical care and discussion. The father's feelings may run from elation to terror or indifference. The medical and nursing staff will themselves be subject to emotional pressures. Dealing continually with 'evacuations' and those considering such an operation must have its impact. These emotional factors are important, for they may be very confused or confusing. They may run along with or in contrast to moral and religious values and hinder the ability to see clearly the issues involved.

It is all too easy in such circumstances for prejudice to arise. Misinformation, old wives' tales, and ignorance, fuel the fires of prejudice and popular misconceptions are difficult to correct. The abortion situation both personally and theoretically is an emotional mine-field. Those who enter the discussion need to be aware of their own emotional responses and those of all involved in the situation. The degree to which the final decision will be affected by such emotional factors will depend on the particular moral and religious outlooks held.

(o) DOCTORS' ATTITUDES

The medical profession is just that—a profession. It has its own standards and expectations in the moral area, as well as being subject to legal limits. As a profession, the history of medical involvement with abortion has been one of concern to safeguard the doctor in relation to the law as well as to do the best for the patients involved. The primary aim of the doctor is to save life. There is therefore little conflict where the life of the woman is at risk. This situation is, however, rare. The doctor is concerned about the welfare and health of his patients and thus, confronted with a request for an abortion, must consider all the possible consequences. There are two main judgements he must make. The first is a medical one. What is the best medical procedure in this case? The second is a legal issue. What does the law permit and forbid in these circumstances? Obviously many doctors will add the dimension of their own consciences and integrity. Am I able personally to participate in this abortion? If the doctor's moral views are such as to give a negative reply, he could appeal to the 'conscience clause' in the Abortion Act (1967). In theory, this is fine; in practice, it is more complex. In a busy ward, with colleagues under pressure, the junior doctor in particular may feel it disloyal to refuse to take his share of such cases. Indeed, some would argue that a Roman Catholic doctor would be best to avoid the specialism of obstetrics and gynaecology altogether. In settings where abortion is common, it is extremely hard for the doctor whose conscience is uneasy about the morality of abortion. For some doctors, such fine moral points are not the essence of the issue. They are primarily practitioners concerned to do the best for their patients. This is ambiguous, for there is a sense in which the foetus falls under the care of the doctor, as well as the woman. As an obstetrician, the doctor will strive to preserve the life of the foetus. As a gynaecologist, practising abortion, the doctor will remove foetal life.

Doctors were agreed on the necessity of some form of abortion law. They played a major part in the framing of its clauses. Many are now concerned that the law requires adaptation (f), especially in light of improvements in the techniques of neo-natal care. This would mean a slight lowering of the age limitation on the performing of abortions, though this depends on early testing both for pregnancy and for deformity. Others are concerned at rumours of financial abuses and would be happy to see more rigid control of private clinics.

However, for the doctor the dilemma often becomes not so much a question of law or of medical expertise, but of how to respond to a woman's plea for an abortion. If abortion on demand is to be avoided, then some criteria must be used. The problem is that few doctors have the time and the expertise to explore fully the social and psychological dimensions within the context of normal clinical hours and settings. Thus doctors may feel at the mercy of the clamant and forceful person demanding an abortion, even when the grounds for such action may be weak. Nevertheless, most doctors would argue strongly for the maintenance of their medical freedom to have the final decision in medical cases.

(p) NURSING ATTITUDES

In the professional sense, the nursing staff share most of the attitudes of the medical profession. In addition, nurses feel that they are called on far more for personal counselling and support by the patient regardless of the abortion decision. The time spent with each patient and the opportunity to build relationships is much greater for the nurse. This, of course, creates greater pressure on the nurse, who may feel that she is left to 'pick up the pieces' in situations where guilt and regret follow an abortion. Some nurses are concerned that abortion seems so easily available to those who do not appear to fall within the categories permitted by law. Some nurses find the task of assisting in and disposing of the aborted foetus unpleasant and distasteful. The nurse is in a difficult position, for she is responsible to the doctor, who manages the patient; yet she deals more directly with the patient. By and large nursing attitudes towards abortion are cautious and conservative, concerned lest the profession's reputation for preserving and caring for life be adversely affected and that the proper safeguards for abortion are not always adhered to properly.

(q) WOMEN'S LIBERATION

For many women the abortion issue has typified their struggle towards freedom and integrity. The forces of women's liberation have been and remain active to safeguard the right of every woman to have an abortion if she chooses. It is woman who is affected by pregnancy and by termination. It is her own body, and she is free to do with it what she will. The pro-abortion case from the women's liberation lobby had negative and positive aspects. Negatively, abortion meant the end of male domination in decision-making; of back-street abortions and the harm done by those to women; of forced weddings on the grounds of pregnancy; of unwanted children in and out of marriage; of having to pay for mistakes and accidents in sex; of suffering further because of sexual abuse; and of defective life and the suffering that brings to the whole of society and the strain and pressure on the woman in particular.

There is also the positive side of the case. Abortion means better life for the woman, her family, and in global terms for a world with one less mouth to feed. Natural abortions occur, so clinical abortion is simply an extension of nature's work. It is safer to have an abortion than to continue with a pregnancy. If a woman feels that her life will be more secure if she has an abortion, then it is her right to have it. The foetus is purely a parasite with no personal or independent life. Indeed, the liberationist is scathing as to the double standards of the religious objectors to abortion. The absence of funeral arrangements, death certificate, and the lesser degree of mourning for the loss of the foetus seems to show that the Church and the state do not really believe in the personhood of the foetus. The protection of the foetus cannot be used as a counterweight to the rights of the woman.

Such strongly expressed arguments have had some degree of success and the recent failure of the Corrie amendment, which attempted to lighten the law on abortion, was hailed as a victory for women and the cause of liberation. Obviously, there has been a genuine revolution in the role and perception of the role of women, not only among women, but in the whole of society. It is not yet clear when or where the process of change will end. Some feel that the case for women's liberation has done its work and is now verging on the lunatic fringe. Others are clear that the work has only begun and more radical changes are called for. The issue of abortion will remain one acid test for women's liberation on its own admission. Any attempts at regressive change will be bitterly opposed. However, such opposition will only be successful if the majority of women support the case and if the justice of that case is evident. Both these caveats are hotly disputed by those who are uneasy about the stridency of women's liberation.

(r)   DEFINITION OF LIFE (see d(ii) above)

(s)   DEFINITION OF A PERSON (see d(iii) above)

(t) DEFINITION AND FORMS OF ABORTION

When it comes to the debate between the opposing sides on abortion, both sides agree that nature aborts spontaneously severely deformed life. However, the glosses on this theme that 'nature does it already' are very different. The pro-abortionist argues that the fact that 'nature does it already' enables us to assist nature in the more safe and secure settings of the hospital ward. In contrast, the anti-abortionist argues that the activity of nature in spontaneous abortion precludes the necessity and propriety of our interference with a natural process. If there are severe problems, nature will deal with them. Obviously many spontaneous abortions do occur at the very early stages of pregnancy, so much so that many women do not even realize that they are pregnant, as the embryo foetus disappears in the monthly menstrual flow. This natural argument runs into problems with the improvement in pre-natal care and the way that medicine can both arrest or support natural processes from the earliest stages of pregnancy.

Clinical abortion may be performed by surgical or chemical means and the use of either a local or general anaesthetic. The procedure itself is relatively straightforward and the likelihood of sterility is extremely rare. What is more debatable is the psychological effect of the abortion. There are many who argue that post-abortive trauma is a common result and is a contra-indication to abortions. Others feel that the extent of such trauma is rare and much less than the likely complications of a continuing pregnancy or indeed of post-natal depression. As we have already seen, there is also disagreement about the level of awareness of the foetus in the performing of an abortion. If a young woman can be tried for maltreating shrimps, it is argued, then how much more should the law concern itself with the 'pain' of the foetus? There needs to be a great deal more clinical work done, before we can rely on the 'facts' in such disputes. It is interesting to note that some moralists are uneasy about the use of the Intra-Uterine Device (IUD) on the grounds that it is an abortifacient (causes an abortion). It certainly ensures that the fertilized egg will not be implanted on the wall of the womb. Whether this constitutes adequate grounds for moral unease about this form of con-traception depends on when we believe human life begins.

(u) MY OWN INVOLVEMENT

It is important in considering the issue of abortion whether this is an academic exercise, a preparation for possible problems, or a response to a particular pastoral problem. In all of these, it is vital that one is clear as to one's role and obligations in the situation. Obviously one must know what one believes. One must be conscious of one's emotional reactions and prejudices and take account of these. One must ask what is one's aim and goal in the particular situation. For many Christian people the likely role will be that of a counsellor. This role is interpreted along two main lines. The first is the non-directive style. The aim here is clarification and assisting those directly involved in the situation to understand both it and themselves and enable them to reach a decision in full awareness of the possible consequences and fully committed to their decision. The alternative model is that of directive counselling. In this the concern is to enable those involved to grasp the practical and moral realities of the situation and to do what is right and offer support in that decision. Naturally, there will be very different views about what is right, even among Christians, and this may be confusing for those involved, if they seek a variety of advice. The fundamental issue here is the freedom of the individual to make his own decision. The degree of pressure applied by the counsellor may lead to different degrees of guilt and unease after the situation has been resolved. Thus the counsellor needs to be clear about what he believes, how he should counsel, as well as the likely consequences of his advice.

(v) CONSEQUENCES c(ii); d(vii); g; m

We have already covered most of the ground under this heading. Consequences matter, but they are not totally predictable and must be balanced by motives and intentions (see Utilitarianism, pp. 32–3). Whether or not an abortion happens, consequences will follow. For the foetus, it will mean life or death. It may mean illegitimacy, being unwanted, severe handicap, or none of these. For the mother it may mean post-abortive trauma, release from anxiety, the full rigours and joys of pregnancy, changes in economic, social and personal relationships, or none of these. The father will also be affected (g) as will other members of the family. The medical and nursing professions may be affected individually and as a profession with a perceived change in their role in society. Would-be adoptive parents will be affected, though one must question the morality of 'producing' children for adoption. It is extremely difficult to be absolute concerning these consequences, as it is to be final about two other consequentialist lines of attack.

The first argues against abortion on the grounds that thereby we are deprived of great men and women. It is not clear how we can know the greatness which will never flower. The other line is the wedge argument. It argues against abortion on the grounds that this will lead to a general weakening of our attitude towards the sanctity of life. Abortions of unwanted foetuses today may lead to the extinction of normal, healthy people on some racial, social or political ground. There is an unjustifiable leap in this argument, which needs support. It may be possible to supply such support, but it is necessary for the consequentialist to produce the goods. Consequences matter, but some are more certain than others and it is to these that attention should be focused.

(w) WHO CHOOSES? a(i)(v); f; g; n; o; q; u

As we come to the end of our list of relevant issues, we see the inter-relationship of so many of the issues and categories. We have examined the claims that the woman should decide, the father, the doctor, the counsellor, or the family and relatives. We have seen the necessity for the interest of the foetus to be defended. In the end, the decision must be made. The real point at issue lies between the medical practitioner and the woman, in the case of conflict. We are all happy when others make decisions when they agree with our views. We are less happy when their decisions differ. Inevitably the medical profession will claim final priority, though this remains subject to law and to professional scrutiny. Others will claim that only the woman herself has an absolute right to make such a decision. Others will feel that the criteria of moral and religious truth should be the basis for the decision regardless of who actually makes it.

This brings us to the crux of the problem for the Christian. Given the massive amount of information which is important in the making of moral decision, how are we to decide between different moral outlooks and emphases? This requires the turning of attention to the first important principles which the Christian holds. To do this may mean firstly, discovering what his (her) moral principles actually are, as well as giving some order of priority to these principles.

2 First important principles

What are the principles the Christian uses when he comes to the issue of abortion? In light of these principles what order of priorities will operate in the decision-making process?

(a) HAS SCRIPTURE SOME PARTICULAR TEACHING ON PRINCIPLES WHICH IS RELEVANT HERE?

(i) Creation
Are there particular principles to be derived from these sources?

1. *Natural law:* When the Christian examines natural law, it is clear that nature's design is that women are naturally equipped to have children both in terms of physical and psychological make-up, and that sexual intercourse is designed as the means of procreation. It is thus natural for intercourse to lead to conception and for women to be pregnant and bear children. It is also natural for spontaneous abortion to occur in some cases of severe abnormality. However, that natural law functions in this way is not the only nor final thing to be said. While it is natural for women to have children, the fertile period of their lives is extremely limited, both in overall span of years and within the terms of the monthly menstrual cycle. This inevitably means that many acts of sexual intercourse have no procreative possibilities. Despite these caveats, it would be difficult to deny that pregnancy and motherhood are natural to womankind.

The natural occurrence of spontaneous abortions is likewise double-edged. As we have seen, this may be used as a ground for the refusal of an abortion or as the basis for an extension of abortive techniques in the safety of sterile settings. Thus the facts from nature still require to be applied on the basis of some other moral grounds. In themselves, they do not necessarily point to a total rejection of abortion; though they do tend to support the anti-abortion position.

2. *Man in the image of God:* God created men and women in his image. He is pictured as breathing his life into mankind. Man is created with spiritual dimensions and to enjoy fellowship with God. Man and woman are part of God's eternal purpose. As we are made in the image of God, our human life is to be reverenced. This is without debate for those who are able to fulfil that relationship. The case of the foetus is more difficult. At what point does the foetus begin to reflect that image of God? Tradition has tended to argue that from the very start of human life, the image of God is present. If, however, the content of the image of God is spiritual capacity and the ability to have a relationship with God, it is clear that the most that can be said is that the foetus has the potential for such capacities, but does not fulfil these totally.

3. *Conscience:* The appeal to Christian conscience tends to be associated with natural law. We should be able to discern the will of God by reference to our consciences, if we are in close relationship with God. The traditional role of conscience has been that life is perceived as sacred and to be preserved almost at all costs. Certainly Christian conscience must be uneasy at any deliberate taking of life. This judgement rests on intuitive certainty. The difficulty is that at the present time many Christian doctors and nurses feel that their consciences will not allow them to see suffering on the part of the woman. This is not only in cases of risk to life and sexual crime, but in certain psychological and social settings. Compassion and mercy are the grounds of appeal and the basis of the conscientious involvement in abortions. At the same time such Christians would confess that there is a real sense of guilt and an awareness of conscience in the destruction of life. If it were possible to act in some other way and preserve the mother's well-being without the loss of foetal life, then that path would be gladly followed. Such conscientious struggle is a major difficulty in seeking to use conscience alone as the final ground of appeal in the abortion decision.

4. *Creation ordinances:* It is clear from the accounts of the creation that man was not only made in the image of God, but was created as steward of life and to live in harmony with his fellow man. God's will is thus discernible as seeking the preservation and nurturing of life and against the destruction of human life. This, of course, leads back to the question of the humanity of foetal life. Nevertheless where life is concerned, man's primary duty is to act as a steward and to preserve his stewardship in responsibility before God.

5. *The Fall:* The account of the Fall is unambiguous in stressing the reality of human sin. We are all affected by sin. This means not only is the world we inhabit a twisted shadow of its true purpose and nature, but also that man and his judgement are impaired. Our decisions are thus liable to be flawed. Decisions about abortion may thus be influenced by selfishness, emotionalism, prejudice, carelessness, and even exploitation. Given the reality of sin, there is a sense in which it is no surprise that abuse of sexuality and the discords of relationships lead to situations where the question of abortion is considered. An awareness of our sin will make the Christian guarded in his judgement and concerned to check his motivation and moral basis. It will also recognize human responsibility for evil and the need to work for forgiveness and renewal.

(ii) The Old Testament

What particular principles may be derived from these sources?

1. *Covenant and Law:* Within the Law, there are strict rules governing the taking of life. Some would argue that within the Decalogue the fifth commandment, 'Thou shalt not kill' (Exod. 20.13) gives a clear indication of God's attitude towards such matters as abortion. This is difficult to sustain for the implied situation is that of murder and it is less than clear that the motives of those engaging in abortions are of murderous intent with the full *mens rea* (criminal mind). It is motives of compassion and concern which move many who are involved.

Yet it is in the following chapter that we have some specific reference to *in utero* life.

> If, when men come to blows, they hurt a woman who is pregnant and she suffers a miscarriage, though she does not die of it, the man responsible must pay the compensation demanded of him by the woman's master; he shall hand it over, after arbitration. But should she die, you shall give life for life, eye for eye, tooth for tooth, hand for hand, foot for foot, burn for burn, wound for wound, stroke for stroke (Exod. 21.22–5, JB).

This shows some distinction between the value of the life of the mother and the life of the foetus. It does not imply that foetal life has no significance. Foetal life matters and is to be preserved. However, the life of the woman is of greater value.

2. *Wisdom Literature:* Within the Psalms there is an important reference to foetal life in the context of praise of God's omniscience.

> It was you who created my inmost self,
> and put me together in my mother's womb;
> for all these mysteries I thank you:
> for the wonder of myself, for the wonder of your works.

> You know me through and through
> from having watched my bones take shape
> when I was being formed in secret,
> knitted together in the limbo of the womb.

> You had scrutinised my every action,
> all were recorded in your book,
> my days listed and determined,
> even before the first of them occurred
> (Ps. 139.13–17, JB).

It is obvious that the psalmist views God's concern for him as stretching back to his life in the womb and that from the earliest moments of life, God's plan and purpose for his life is seen as already existing even before his birth. On such a basis, the foetus would seem to be of vital significance to God and accordingly ought to be so for us.

3. *The Prophets:* This same sense of the significance of foetal life is evident in two of the major prophets as they reflect on their prophetic callings. Isaiah in one of the servant songs records:

> And now Yahweh has spoken,
> he who formed me in the womb to be his servant,
> to bring Jacob back to him,
> to gather Israel to him:
> (Isa. 49.5, JB).

In more personal terms Jeremiah dates his calling as a prophet in the following terms:

> The word of Jahweh was addressed to me, saying,
> 'Before I formed you in the womb I knew you;
> before you came to birth I consecrated you;
> I have appointed you as prophet to the nations'.
> (Jer. 1.4–5, JB).

God is intimately concerned for life within the womb, for that life is seen as playing a vital part in the purposes of God.

(iii) The New Testament

What principles may be derived from these sources?

1. *Redemption:* For the Christian the only solution to the power of sin and the Fall is through redemption. This is not so much within the power of man, but is God's gift mediated to the world through the living, dying and rising again of his Son, Jesus Christ. That process of redemption is, however, only begun in the here and now. Its final completion awaits the fulfilment of the purposes of God. The possibility of redemption means that the dominion of sin is neither total nor final. The power of God may be brought into every situation of sin and its consequences. However, this is not necessarily the path to some simple solution, for the path of redemption is by way of the cross and of suffering. The Christian is called to share in the suffering of the world and to seek to alleviate the effects of suffering and of sin. This is a call to be involved in the complexities of abortion situations, realizing that suffering will be involved.

2. *Kingdom ethics:* The most specific reference relevant to the issue of abortion occurs in the setting of the context for the coming of Christ. When the angel Gabriel visited Mary, she is greeted by a promise:

> Listen! You are to conceive and bear a son, and you must name him Jesus. He will be great and will be called Son of the Most High. The Lord God will give him the throne of his ancestor David; he will rule over the House of Jacob for ever and his reign will have no end (Luke 1.32–3, JB).

It is clear that even before the conception of Christ, the ministry that he will exercise is already fixed and clear. This same awareness of the significance of the foetal Christ is represented in the meeting of Elizabeth and Mary.

> Now as soon as Elizabeth heard Mary's greeting, the child leapt in her womb and Elizabeth was filled with the Holy Spirit. She gave a loud cry and said, 'Of all women you are most blessed, and blessed is the fruit of your womb. Why should I be honoured with a visit from the mother of my Lord? For the moment your greeting reached my ears, the child in my womb leapt for joy' (Luke 1.41–4, JB).

The foetal John is recorded as responding at the six-month stage to the presence of the pregnant Mary and the presence of the Saviour in the womb. As with the prophets, the foetus within the womb has a crucial role to play in the purposes of God—the salvation of the world.

3. *Paul's ethics* } There are no specific references to foetal life
4. *Pastoral Epistles* } to help us. Life is seen in the context of God and it is more the end of life than the beginning that is the New Testament's concern.

(b) HAS TRADITION SOME PARTICULAR TEACHING OR PRINCIPLES WHICH ARE RELEVANT HERE?

Traditionally the Church has shown great concern for the preservation of life. By using the various biblical passages a strong doctrine of the importance of foetal life has developed. This found focus in the classical debate over 'ensoulment'. This was the attempt to define the precise moment when the foetus became a living soul. Like the definition of when human life begins, the various alternatives were hotly disputed (see pp. 95–6). The danger of the traditional debate was a dualism which separated the material and biological from the spiritual. It was as if God came along and added a spiritual dimension to a physical existence. Such dualistic thought is rejected today and the focus of tradition stresses the significance of foetal life from the earliest moment possible. That foetal life has spiritual dimensions, though exactly what these are is unclear. The attack on this view suggests that it results in a view of a heaven containing rows and rows of half-formed foetuses aborted either spontaneously or by medical techniques. Such a caricature is in danger of missing the point both of the metaphorical language of heaven and of the spiritual dimension of the foetus. If there is such a dimension, it implies that we should treat foetal life with reverence and seek to preserve what was created for fellowship with God.

(c) HAS THE SPIRIT OR THE CHURCH SOME PARTICULAR TEACHING OR PRINCIPLES WHICH ARE RELEVANT HERE?

The Church as a whole is of one mind in its concern for the abuse of abortion and the need to protect the innocent lives of the foetuses. Nevertheless, there is division among Christians about whether or not abortion is ever permissible. Both views claim the validation of the Spirit as the ground of their view. The Roman Catholic view is extremely uneasy about the possibility of abortion. Life is to be preserved at all costs, for life is sacred. We have seen the law of double effect (see p. 108) and how this makes abortion possible in very extreme cases. Such exceptions in no way affect the central point of the Roman view. The Spirit is calling Christians to defend the rights and existence of the child within the womb in a society which has become careless of life itself.

In contrast, the typical Protestant view, while accepting the sanctity of life, would lay emphasis on the sinful world in which we live. Given the reality of sin, we must make decisions which are the lesser of two evils. In extreme situations of rape, incest, extreme deformity, and genuine psychological breakdown, abortion is permissible. The Christian virtues of compassion and mercy are to be shown by the power of the Spirit. If this is sinful, we are to sin boldly, for this is to share in the suffering and redemption of the world. Such views are in no way a charter for abortion on demand. Life is sacred and to be preserved, but not at all costs. Each case is to be determined on its merits.

Having outlined the principles as expressed in Scripture, tradition, the Church and through the Spirit, we are left with the question of what to do with them. At the one extreme some may feel that the cultural gap between the present age and that of the writing of the Scriptures is so great that we cannot apply teaching for those settings to the moral issues of today. The same line of argument follows with the traditional debates. The problem with such an extreme is that it cuts off present-day Christianity from its biblical and historical roots. It assumes that the Church today will make decisions under the power of the Spirit which bear no relation to the perceived guidance of the Spirit through the ages. It is difficult to be sure that our present perceptions are so much better than those of the past. Nevertheless, if the concern is to ensure that the present-day aspects of the moral dilemmas are taken seriously, this is vital. However, it is still necessary to refer our moral judgements to our first important principles.

In examining these principles it is clear that there are two main ones. The first is the sanctity of life. The second is the Christian's duty to be compassionate. In deciding which is the first principle, it is obvious that Christians will disagree over emphasis, but not that both principles should be observed. For most cases there will be no divergence between the principles and Christians will be able to agree. In rare cases, conflict may ensue and Christians then must be firmly convinced in their own minds in the context of the Christian community. (See above, p. 57). The question in such exceptional circumstances is simple. Is life to be preserved at all costs?

3 Aims, goals and objectives

Having derived our basic principles and clarified their priority, we must then ask what our objectives are in the situation confronting us. If we assume a counselling situation, we must ask what is our role, what is desirable, what is actually possible, what motives are at work, and what will the consequences be of any decision reached. These aims are directly related to our first principles. In seeking to preserve life, we would be looking for ways to help the woman, the father and the medical staff to preserve that life. In seeking to offer compassion, we would try to take account of the pressures of the past, present and future situations. How far we push our principles depends on our perception of our role. If the advice is non-directive, the main goal will be to help those involved make their own decision fully aware of motives and consequences. If the advice is more directive, we should be seeking to advocate our principles as forcefully as possible, without doing harm to the integrity of those concerned. We have considered already the factors of motivation and consequences.

However, there is another goal for the Christian beyond dealing with the specific problem. It is to deal with the conditions which lead to the possibility and necessity for abortion. This goes back to the failures in human relationships and to misuses of sexual expression. The Christian should be aiming so to change people's understanding of life, relationships and sexuality, that the problem of abortion will diminish. This will mean both a dealing with sin and a process of education. People need to be educated, but they also require to be changed. Christians, alone and together, will be engaged in this work and that may mean active support of legal changes and pressure groups. The true mark of having a goal is that we seek to fulfil the goal. Our goals are evident in what we do and what we fail to do.

4 Alternatives, possibilities, choices

In counselling women in the abortion situation, there is often their strong feeling that there is only one thing they can do. One task of the counsellor (regardless of moral or religious outlook) is to consider other possibilities in the situation. Obviously, there can be an abortion and the consequences of that decision must be explored. If, however, the woman is uneasy about an abortion, there are the possibilities of adoption and of trying to keep the child. Adoption means both the completion of the pregnancy and the bringing of great happiness to those who long to be parents but are unable so to do. This decision will require great help both during the pregnancy and in the traumatic days of parting with the baby. To continue the pregnancy and keep the child may be hard for both the married and unmarried mother. We have seen the possible effects in social, economic, physical and psychological terms on her, on the child, and on others in the situation. Yet it should be possible to choose life and to know that in handicap or normality there will be personal, church and government resources to draw upon. It is with the genuineness of these alternatives that the Christian needs to reflect carefully. Are we truly prepared to supply these resources and to meet these needs not only in the short term? People will only consider alternatives where it is clear that there will be the necessary help to carry them through.

5 Other people's viewpoints

It is all too easy to bulldoze people with our own views. The proper moral decision is taken when other people have been taken seriously. This means listening to the other viewpoints, and indeed, even suggesting other such viewpoints to people in the situation. This is not to confuse them, but to try and guarantee that their decision is properly informed. For the anti-abortionist to pretend that the pro-abortionist has nothing to say does violence to the integrity of both views. People will disagree and those disagreements may be expressed. At this point, however, it is vital to take people beyond the disagreement to the crucial principles at stake. Then those involved must make their decision. At least, it will be as fully informed as possible.

Conclusion

If people are looking for the one answer, they will feel cheated. My aim is to clarify how people should reach their own decision, rather than to propound mine. This process of reaching such decisions is rare, yet it is vital that we know how to proceed when we are confronted with moral dilemmas. The issue of abortion does not confront most of us every day. Yet it is important to know what we think. By going through the clarificatory process above, it should be possible to decide one's own position and to know the alternatives.

6
Matters of Life and Death: (2) Euthanasia

The definition of 'euthanasia' is 'dying well'. This has come to be associated with means of helping patients to die. As we approach the issue we must stress the object of this particular exercise is to clarify what is involved in making moral decisions concerning euthanasia. We are not dealing with a specific example seeking one solution. Rather we are seeking to understand the nature of the moral dilemma, the principles involved, and to form an adequate basis for the taking of a moral decision in this area. To do this, we follow the method previously applied (see previous chapter).

1   C.A.F. (Consider all the factors)

One helpful tool is to list as many topics as possible which we think relate to this issue, as quickly as possible. We can thus add or subtract from the list, as other things occur. As we have already seen, working our way through such a list enables us to group various themes together. The list helps ensure no vital aspects of the problem are omitted.

    A. Definition of euthanasia
    B. Link to suicide
    C. Active versus passive euthanasia
    D. Problem of ageing
    E. Care of the dying
    F. Definitions of life and death

G. Rights
H. Patient
I. Family and relatives
J. Medical and nursing staff
K. Pain and suffering
L. The importance of personality
M. Finance
N. Medical techniques and their limits
O. Legislation
P. Value and definition of a person
Q. Who decides?
R. Consequences
S. Public opinion
T. Alternatives
U. Fears and emotions
V. Moral and religious values
W. Compassion
X. World-wide context
Y. Deformity and handicap

Each of these will be examined in turn, seeking to draw attention to the interconnections between categories. By such a means, we shall be well informed as to the issues at stake.

A. DEFINITION OF EUTHANASIA

While in strictly definitional terms, 'euthanasia' means 'good death', it has become almost exclusively applied to the deliberate ending of life, with the desire to avoid pain. It is the legalized killing by a doctor of someone who is suffering from an incurable disease. This legalized killing takes place at the free and rational request of the patient. Thus we are concerned with *voluntary euthanasia* rather than *compulsory*. The patient has expressed the desire to die, under specified circumstances. Such a procedure is not the same as the switching off of a heart-lung machine where death has already occurred. Nor is it strictly speaking the same situation as when a doctor may prescribe powerful drugs to alleviate pain, but these may have serious and even fatal side-effects. This is another example of the Law Of Double Effect, where the doctor is concerned to alleviate pain by giving necessary pain-killing drugs. Eventually such drugs require fatal doses to do their work. Nor does voluntary euthanasia include cases where someone takes the life of a child, the mentally disturbed, or an elderly person, who are all unable to offer resistance or to make any choice in the situation. Euthanasia thus refers not simply to the desire we all share to die as pleasantly as possible, but to the legal opportunity of assisted suicide.

B.   LINK TO SUICIDE

There is some confusion between euthanasia and suicide. The law does not now regard the committing of suicide as a criminal offence, whereas the assisting of someone to death is a criminal act. Suicide is self-destruction. It is the direct and deliberate taking of one's own life. Of course, there may be a similarity between suicide and euthanasia in the motives involved. The desire to escape from intolerable pain or from hopeless situations, as well as concern to alleviate the burden on family and friends, may well be common motivations in both cases. A further distinction needs to be drawn between euthanasia (and indeed suicide) and the willing surrender of one's life. Confusingly this is sometimes referred to as suicide, whereas it is rather martyrdom. For the martyr death is not the aim. If he could perform the same act without his own death, then he would do so. He does not *will* his own death, but is prepared to die. He is prepared to accept death as the unavoidable, unfortunate consequence of performing an act of charity, justice, mercy and piety.

> Captain Oates left his companions in the Antarctic because he had become an hindrance to them. He did not want to kill himself. He had struggled too far for that. He was not a quitter, but recognised that he could go no further and was horrified to realise that if he remained in the shelter, his friends would refuse to leave. He walked out into the snow, not to kill himself, but to try to give his friends a better chance of life. He did not kill himself. The snow, blizzard and frostbite did that. He was no suicide. This is easy to misunderstand. If he had shot himself, then his death would

have been suicide. But I cannot believe that everyone who 'lays down his life for his friends' is a suicide. (From my article 'Human Suicide and Para-suicide', *C.M.F. Guideline No. 64.*)

Or course, there will be some dissent from the pro-euthanasia camp, who will suggest that some who request euthanasia do so for the sake of family and friends rather than for the self-seeking motive of avoiding pain. This may well be so, though it is difficult to ensure the purity of motives in such cases and, more importantly, the plea for euthanasia involves the responsibility of taking life to fall on someone else's shoulders. Such assisted suicide is quite different from being put to death or dying for the sake of others.

C. ACTIVE VERSUS PASSIVE EUTHANASIA

One further necessary distinction in the euthanasia debate is between what is called active and passive euthanasia. Active euthanasia is when death is caused *directly* by a third party in response to a specific request from a patient. It is to kill. In contrast, passive euthanasia is the description for cases where various forms of treatment to prolong life are withheld. Some would doubt, if it is correct in such cases to refer to euthanasia at all. Examples of such cases would be not beginning treatment, when death is the alternative or allowing the patient to die when the death process is already well-established. The poet Arthur Hugh Clough expresses the difference neatly: 'Thou shalt not kill; but needst not strive officiously to keep alive'. Many, including the medical profession, are concerned at the lengths to which procedures are taken to maintain life, when there is no real prospect of any genuine well-being or quality of life (see N, F). Killing is different from allowing someone to die in circumstances where there is no hope of improvement. In this sense, death is a natural process rather than an obtrusive medical one. When we are discussing euthanasia, we are referring to active euthanasia and all that this entails in terms of the patient's request and the doctor's acquiescence.

D. THE PROBLEMS OF AGEING

All too often the question of euthanasia is associated with the elderly. Though euthanasia is relevant to incurable disease at every stage in life, the problems of ageing pose particular difficulty. The very fact that Britain has an increasing aged population means that the balance of society is changing. There are more older and fewer younger people. At the same time people are living longer because of improvements in social and medical terms. We have the capacity to maintain life for long periods. Diseases which formerly affected the elderly, like pneumonia, may be controlled fairly easily. Old age, however, brings a host of problems. First and foremost, the elderly person may find a diminishing of powers. When such a person is no longer as fit as formerly, even simple tasks may become difficult. The elderly may become confused, senile, incontinent and unable to care for themselves. They may feel degraded and that life retains no dignity. Often in such circumstances, the old become totally dependent on family or friends, and that creates pressure on both single and married children to care for aged parents. Very often this is construed as a choice between allowing the old person to suffer or the family to be deprived. The other extreme is also common. That is where the elderly person has no remaining friends or relatives and is alone and without the social resources most of us take for granted.

In all such situations, it is not uncommon for the question to be asked, 'What is there to look forward to?' The answer often seems a pattern of growing dependence and degeneration till total helplessness results. This, some feel, is the demise of all dignity. Obviously not all older people are in these circumstances, but a growing number are, and we must take note of this fact. Obviously the local and national government take responsibility through the medical and social services for the care of the elderly, but such care is dependent on the skills and finance available. Within medicine, geriatrics is often a 'cinderella' area in terms of teaching, practice, and national health service finance. The myriad of urgent social problems facing the social services can mean that the time and care given to the senior citizens is small in proportion to their needs. Though they have given much to the nation, they have all too often the feeling of being left on the scrapheap to rot. It is little wonder that the subject of euthanasia both excites fear on the part of the vulnerable elderly and also offers a solution to what seems an intractable problem. Euthanasia may offer death with dignity.

E. CARE OF THE DYING

One of the key factors in resistance to the necessity for euthanasia comes from the hospice movement. The picture of ageing alone was matched by the process of dying in people's minds. Death involved great pain, and incurable disease meant unbearable pain. Death was also a great conspiracy of silence. No one knew they were dying. They might guess, but medical and nursing staff seemed at pains to be optimistic and positive. Relatives and friends put brave faces on at visiting times, and patients knew better than to ask if they were dying. Ordinary hospital wards were the setting for death with no privacy and little opportunity to retain any vestige of dignity. People prayed for a quick and painless death.

The hospice movement has changed much of that. It has created an environment, where the secrecy and, with that, the fear of death has been diminished. Specially trained medical and nursing staff have given patients the time they require for understanding their situation and coming to terms with it. For most people, it is not so much death itself which is fearful, but the pain of dying. The hospice movement has focused attention on the area of pain control. It is possible so to regulate drugs that the patient may be free from pain without being totally under the influence of the drug. All too often patients were reduced to zombies or made drug-addicts, when such over-prescription of medication was unnecessary. Assured that dying need not be painful, people have been better able to come to terms with the experience of and anticipation of death. Of course, such care and provision are extremely costly in terms of resources and staffing. At a time of inflation and financial restriction, there is unease about launching major expenditure in the area of new hospitals. Yet the hospice movement flourishes and provides a setting for care of the dying, which is a real alternative to the path of euthanasia.

F. DEFINITIONS OF LIFE AND DEATH

In the previous chapter we examined the medical and spiritual questions of when life begins and the definition of a person (see pp. 95–7). Our attention here will focus on the definition of death. Roughly speaking, traditional definitions of death centred on the absence of respiration and heartbeat. If you stopped breathing and your heart stopped, you were dead. Modern techniques of resuscitation have made such definitions inadequate, and so attention has shifted to brain death. The absence of certain patterns of brain waves measured on an EEG (electro-encephalo-graph) is used as the measure of the presence or absence of life. Obviously as medical techniques are refined, the moment of death will be more accurately measured, but that still leaves us with the difficult cases. A personal example may help to clarify. I was recalled from holiday to the bedside of my mother in hospital. She looked well, she was a good colour, and her body rose and fell in the steady rhythm of breathing. She seemed asleep and at any moment likely to open her eyes to say, 'Hello'. The doctors said that she was dead. Her brain had been destroyed by a massive haemorrhage. The next day, after further checks, the heart/lung machine was switched off and she was officially pronounced dead. For people who are unconscious the medical expert is called on to pass judgement as to the likelihood of a return to consciousness. In such cases there may be a return to life, but doubt must be raised as to the nature of that life.

In traditional terms this is expressed as the tension between quality and quantity of life. A person may continue to exist as a vegetable totally dependent on artificial means for survival and be unconscious with no prospect of regaining that consciousness. Immediately there are those who will raise doubts as to the accuracy of such medical prognostications. New medical dis-coveries may happen. Spontaneous recovery may occur. The truly difficult examples are often found among the severely deformed and handicapped. Recent publicity has focused on the problem of such cases at the neo-natal stage. What quality of life is possible for a severely handicapped child? Should medical science be used to try to continue a life, the quality of which leaves much to be desired? Should parents and medical and nursing staff be put through the agony of such procedures, when there will be so little improvement to show for the effort expended? Should the young child be forced to endure yet more pain, when there is no real hope of well-being and of pain-free existence? Such questions are difficult and force us to ask 'when is a person a person?' How are we to deal with those who will never (again) be able to respond in human relationships, be capable of rational conduct, or be free from artificial life-support systems? Are we to prolong their lives or to put an end to them?

Many would agree that such cases are nothing to do with euthanasia, for these are not situations where choice is possible on the patient's part. Nevertheless 'mercy-killing' may be the appropriate term. Certainly doctors already do make decisions, which are matters of life and death. While we may not wish to remove or unduly restrict such decision-making, it is clear that there must be some safeguards on the judgement of the doctor.

Definitions of life and death in the area of euthanasia centre on the degree of responsive, meaningful, thoughtful life which is possible for an individual. For those who feel that even these basic facets of well-being are denied them, the freedom to choose death is claimed as a right. The issue of such claims will be dealt with below, but the situation where such claims cannot be made, though merciful release is an option, remains an area where medical practice must be subject to adjudication without being hampered in its clinical judgements.

G. RIGHTS

The Voluntary Euthanasia Society argues for euthanasia on the basis of rights. The patient, it is claimed, has the right and the freedom to choose death. The patient has the right to die when and where he wants. Part of this is the claim of the right to death with dignity avoiding painful and distressing processes which are liable to reduce a human being to the level of a dependent vegetable. There is a feeling of oddity about such a right, for death is an inevitable process. We all die sooner or later, whether we like it or not. Part of the claim for this right rests on the advances of medical technology. Life processes may be prolonged artificially, thus prolonging the act of dying. The patient may fear such a long drawn-out death. A second aspect of the claim for rights is part of a much larger concern with human rights in every area of life, Western liberation has so emphasized the rights of the individual, that we have come to believe that we should be masters of our own fate. After all, it is my life, why should I not end it if I wish? Modern drugs have made pain unnecessary. We have therefore grown intolerant of the discomfort of pain. Suffering is to be avoided above all costs. Unless life is happy, it is not worth living. Thus the right to die is part of a wider utilitarian view of life and the place of pleasure in that life. Each of these points might be debated separately, but there is a more fundamental problem with the idea of the right to die. Rights imply responsibilities. The right to die implies the responsibility of someone to take life. Killing again is the difference between euthanasia and suicide. Others are involved. Is it proper and just to *require* others to kill us, for this is exactly what the right to die implies? This right to die would inevitably infringe the rights of others, requiring them to do something which ought not to be required of anyone. The justice and indeed the procedure of managing such a right and decision to die (see O) is extremely hazardous and doubtful. Indeed the right to die may be contrasted with the right to life. No one wishes the spectre of compulsory death or euthanasia. We have the right to live, but this right fits oddly with the claim for the right to die. It does not seem possible to hold both rights together, yet this is essentially the position based on the freedom of the individual to choose.

However, the patient whether handicapped, elderly, or incurably ill has certain rights. These are the right to be treated with respect, to have the best treatment available, to be treated honestly, to have privacy and dignity maintained, and to have pain relieved, as far as is possible. These are no new claims. They are part and parcel of all good practice of medicine. Medical and nursing staff are constantly seeking ways of avoiding dehumanizing and depersonalizing forms of care and treatment. However in this context of the rights of the patient and the responsibilities of the medical staff, there must arise the rights of the doctor to cooperation and trust. The doctors and nurses ought not to be subjected to unreasonable demands, expectations and behaviour.

This further area of rights should be noted. The family and relatives of the patient, whether this be a severely handicapped, an elderly, or an incurably ill person, have the right to be informed of all relevant details of care, prognosis and treatment. There is a right too to avoid the pressure of apparently looking to relatives to make decisions which they are ill-equipped to form (Q). The second area of right lies with society as a whole. Society has the right to protect people from themselves, as well as from each other. This is both a responsibility and a right. It means that there are some things society will not allow one member to do to him (herself) or to another. Society has the right to interfere. Thus legislation and public opinion are powerful forces in safeguarding the lives and the care of those facing death (O, S). Obviously these safeguards tend to be aimed at ensuring there is no abuse of the medical and nursing care, but there is also considerable outcry, if public examples of euthanasia in homes are discovered.

H. PATIENT

In turning to the patient, it is clear that the variety of cases and circumstances will be great. Some will be able to reflect rationally with ease, while others may have few signs of rational functions. In the case of the very young, the severely handicapped, the mentally disturbed and the senile, such patients require more careful treatment and safeguards. Both because of what they were, and might yet be, and also what they were meant to be as human beings, such vulnerable forms of human existence deserve our compassion and care. This rules out all forms of compulsory euthanasia. We shall consider further what to do in cases where a previous decision was taken for euthanasia, when in a rational setting (O, Q).

The situation where there is a desire on the part of a patient for euthanasia must be taken seriously. For some the request itself will be a sign of mental instability, but this is to jump to conclusions too quickly. Why should someone want to die by euthanasia? Obviously it will occur largely in settings where the patient is unable to commit suicide. If it is death at all costs, then most people can find ways of killing themselves. To ask for help in such a project, suggests either doubt concerning its wisdom and therefore the need for some reassurance, or else incapacity to perform the desired end. The first motive is self-centred. Such a phrase is meant neutrally. It means the motive is concerned with a person's self. Such a person may be in great pain or facing the prospect of great pain. He or she may have lived a satisfying life and fear increasing debility and failure of physical and mental powers. The person may have had an unhappy life and seek an end to that. He or she may feel that they have outlived their usefulness, have no worth, and are a drain on the relatives, friends and others. This last feeling shifts the motive from the self-centred to the other-centred. Some may seek euthanasia not so much for their own sakes, as for the benefit of others, especially family and friends. This request may be a refusal to be a burden to others.

In dealing with these different kinds of motives, it is important to discover what degree of pain, disability and sense of worthlessness is involved. This means careful listening, counselling and exploration of alternatives. Unless the patient is presented with alternatives, there may be a feeling of being cheated and even grimmer determination to die. In the case of the other-centred motives, it is important to explore the feelings and situations of the others. This is extremely delicate. Knowledge that euthanasia has been contemplated by a relative may add guilt and distress to individuals and families already under pressure. Nevertheless it is vital to clear carefully the patient's perception of the nature and extent of being a burden on others. All too often this may be more a purely personal reflection than an objective reality. It is the task of the medical and social services to seek to alleviate situations where there is genuine burden and distress. Such care and intervention may be both long and short-term, but is vital.

The key issues for patients contemplating euthanasia appear to be a sense of worth, the problem of pain and diminishing powers, and the sense of dependency on others (P, K, U, I, E).

I. FAMILY AND RELATIVES

We have seen some situations where there are no relatives or family left. Here we concentrate on situations, where there are relatives. Selecting from the cases of neo-nates, the severely deformed, the mentally unstable, the elderly and the incurably ill, we shall look at three of these as typical examples. If parents discover that their new-born baby is severely handicapped, this is a major trauma. Guilt, fear and distress are mingled. What is to be done? Doctors will carefully and, we hope, sensitively, explain the nature of the deformity and the likely outcome. There may be little hope of improvement in the condition, and the life-span of the new baby may be limited. But in most cases, there are medical techniques available which will prolong life, treat some of the symptoms, guard against other infections and diseases, and may improve greatly or just slightly the quality of life. In such an emotional situation, where the parents may find it hard to grasp what is said and its significance, the doctor carries great responsibility. How he presents the facts to the parents may well frame the final decision. Obviously where there are strong moral and religious beliefs, the doctor must respect these. Yet the actual practice of doctors does vary from hospital to hospital. Some will struggle valiantly for the slightest chance of improving the quality of life, while others will allow 'nature to take its course'. This phrase is highly misleading. Almost all of medical practice interferes with nature. Such interference may be a speeding up or reinforcing of the path nature might take, for example, in healing, but it is still interference. Most often we find such interference extremely welcome and have grown to depend on it. Now medical science and technology is able to outdo much of nature's work and, in particular, to preserve lives of extremely handicapped children. But should this be so? Is it fair to inflict pain and suffering on the child? Is it just to add to the burden of guilt and unhappiness of the parents by forcing them, or encouraging them to cope with severe abnormality and early death? Is it proper to use valuable financial, medical and nursing resources on cases where the quality of life is so poor? Yet these questions may be matched by another set. Is it just to destroy innocent life? Is it fair to deprive parents of their child's life and add to their guilt and distress by allowing death? Can a doctor cease to preserve human life? Ought not medical science to do its very best, knowing what great new strides may be just around the corner? Who is able to tell what the quality of life really is to the handicapped person? Better some life than no life at all.

Parents will explore all these questions and many more in the situation of neo-natal deformity. Yet that still leaves the issue of who is to decide on what action will be taken (see Q). Whoever decides, the parents' feelings and beliefs are very important.

Examples of the situation with regard to relatives are also found among the elderly. In the previous section we saw the way in which the old person may feel that he (she) is a burden to relatives. In truth, this may be the case. It is vital to meet with and visit the family and relatives to see the kinds of pressure they are under and to gauge the difference that caring for an old person makes to the situation. Families do feel guilty about ageing relatives. They recognize a debt to and love for parents in particular, but often have financial and living circumstances which make care difficult. All too often, single people in particular feel trapped in the care of ageing parents and there seems no escape. Euthanasia does offer a possible solution, but it is fraught with difficulties for families and relatives. Who is to decide? Who would be able to live with the guilt? Is the kind of pressure so great that killing (even of the legalized kind) is permissible? In contrast, families may see older relatives suffering in great pain and diminishing in mental and physical capacities. They may have often talked along the lines of 'when I'm old and alone, just put me to sleep'. Some may feel that they ought to assist the elderly, especially if the request for euthanasia is repeated and forceful. Yet society and the law must protect people from each other and from their own judgements. This is especially the case, where mixed motives are possible. In relieving the pain and distress of an ageing relative, I may inherit a tidy sum. Who can be sure of the purity of motives in such cases?

The first example is that of the incurably ill. The burden of pain may be intolerable to the patient, but so, too, is watching the suffering of a loved one. The strain of caring for the incurably ill may be very great both physically and emotionally. Seeing someone waste away is extremely distressing. What makes it worse, is that there seems no likely improvement or immediate end to the suffering or to the necessity of care. It is all too easy for families to be utterly exhausted by the situation. Small wonder a request for release from pain by euthanasia seems a tempting proposal. Yet is it right to take life? On the other hand, does not compassion mean that we must relieve the agony of another? Without the possibility of an alternative, the choice seems very stark. The alternatives of social and medical aid, professional counselling for family and for patient, and the safety-net of the hospice movement, which has wide domiciliary services, are vital to the family and relatives of the incurably ill. Their own moral and religious beliefs and their relationship with the medical practitioner are also important in discussing any request for euthanasia.

J. MEDICAL AND NURSING STAFF (see also N)

The medical profession is generally fiercely opposed to the principle of voluntary euthanasia. Both the British and World Medical Associations have specifically rejected such a policy. The natural impulse of doctors and nurses is to heal and preserve life. Any pressure on this major role is to be resisted. Once doctors and nurses seemed to be in the business of death control, the sensitive relationship of doctor and patient would be undermined. The phrase, 'I'm just going to put you to sleep now', would strike terror in the helpless patient. Medical staff fear that any legislation for euthanasia would undermine the trust patients feel towards doctors. Already, there is unease in the public's mind concerning organ transplants, using donor organs. This is partly a fear about the timing and definition of death, as well as a nagging doubt as to whether everything possible was done. Nationally and locally there are strict guidelines and checks to safeguard in these situations. Voluntary euthanasia legislation would be likely to affect the situation adversely.

Moreover, the medical profession is uneasy concerning euthanasia legislation in other ways. We have seen the tag, 'Thou shalt not kill; but needst not strive officiously to keep alive'. Doctors do make decisions of life and death. They have to. They are faced with the necessity for instant response to various possibilities and limited resources. Not all kidney or heart patients may have transplants. Apart from the unsuitability of patient and donor, there are not sufficient transplant organs to meet every case. The doctor must decide who is most likely to benefit and he must act accordingly. It is the same with the definition of death. This is a clinical judgement and is made with great care, yet must be made by a medically qualified person. Doctors and their professional organizations are cautious of any form of legislation which is likely to impinge on a doctor's professional judgement. Too careful legislation will mean delay in medical action and make the task of the doctor more difficult and vulnerable. While recognizing the high ethical standards of the profession and the degree of professional control, it is still proper to look for some check on the overkeen practitioner (see N). But while some feel uneasy that doctors may treat life too lightly if euthanasia were to be legalized, there is also the opposite danger.

In dealing with extreme cases, the doctor may go to extraordinary lengths to seek to preserve life at all costs (see N). Death has become a mark of failure for some doctors and to be resisted at all costs. There are limits to what medicine can and ought to do. Doctors alone may not be the best judges of where these limits lie.

When doctors and nurses are dealing with the extreme cases of handicap and incurable illness, it is vital that there should be not only an atmosphere of compassionate care, but also a sense of scrupulous honesty. Of course, how the truth is told affects how readily we are able to cope with that truth, and medical and nursing staff need help and encouragement in these kinds of skills. For some the kind of treatment doctors sometimes give comes into the category of the Law of Double Effect. Dangerous drugs may be given because this is necessary to alleviate pain. The double effect of such drug giving is that not only is pain relieved, but death may ensue. Recent work in pain control has improved this area of practice but more work remains to be done. Nevertheless, in the last analysis, the dosage and treatment are matters of medical judgement and must be left to the doctor with all the professional safeguards intact.

All too often we underestimate the effect of death and dying on medical and nursing staff. This must be both painful and distressing. If we were to legalize euthanasia and require medical staff to be the ministers of such acts, the guilt and distress would be likely to increase greatly. Euthanasia would be an intolerable burden for many doctors and nurses.

K. PAIN AND SUFFERING

For many people it is not death itself which terrifies, but the thought of pain. If death had no pain, people would feel less afraid. This seems especially true in our own sanitized society, where all traces of discomfort are removed by a galaxy of pain-killers. Medical science in curbing pain, has made us more afraid than ever of pain. At the same time, suffering, whether one's own or that of a loved one is impossible for us to understand. Suffering defies reason. We feel helpless in its face. If there were some purpose, it might be easier to accept, but in most cases there seems no point at all. We shall see in the Christian tradition attempts to view suffering in a positive light (V, F, P). In the end there remains some suffering which cannot be explained and which destroys people and lives. We all fear such suffering, and the great killers of our age are often associated with extreme pain.

Thus the avoidance of pain is a key motive in the request for euthanasia. This pain may be the patient's own or the pain they feel they are causing to others by their own condition. There are problems with this. The first is that pain is subjective. Different people are able to face differing amounts of pain. We would hesitate to take someone's life to escape minor pain. Yet what counts as minor or major pain? How is pain to be measured? Though subjective pain is still real to the patient, that pain may be controlled. Modern drugs and forms of treatment are enabling more refined control of pain. People need not suffer. Indeed some, who are responsible for pain clinics, suggest that the age of pain is past. We will soon have a pain-free society, if we want. That rider is important, for pain is a useful warning sign. The same ability to feel pain is likewise an ability to feel pleasure. If we remove one, the other may be affected. When a request is made for euthanasia, the pain must be treated, and if it is possible to discover some meaning to the suffering endured, this may transform the patient.

L. THE IMPORTANCE OF PERSONALITY

(i) Dignity (P)

We have already seen how the patient has a right to be treated with dignity. This means both in terms of care and of forms of treatment, the dignity of the person must be preserved. But dignity is often based on worth and value.

(ii) The value of a person

How much is a person worth? We usually answer that by reference to a will. A person is worth what they leave behind. For others, worth is associated with a person's contribution to society. Their value is the loss they would be, if they died. For others, value depends on one's self and view of oneself. It is the belief in who and what we are. We may make our own estimate of our true self-worth. For the Christian, true value does not lie in either self-estimates or other people's estimates of us. Such a functional view of value is selfish. It is also exclusive. For those with little self-appreciation or with little or no contribution to make to society, either of these bases of worth would mean being of no value at all. For the Christian, value comes from God (see F, I, P). For the humanist, value may simply lie in being human and a person. That is the source of value and there is no need for some other basis than that. It is clear that a sense of value (and often that means our ability to contribute) is a strong element in the consideration of euthanasia. But that still leaves the problem of who will decide what worth is and how much is to be assigned to each person.

(iii) The definition of a person

In Chapter 5 we looked at attempts to define the nature of a person (pp. 96–7). For some this lies in the capacity for rational thought, responsibility or the capacity to form and maintain human relationships. This does create problems for the severely mentally handicapped, young children and the senile. Children we hold to be persons in the making and they are treated as persons because of what is to come in terms of responsibility and rationality. The senile might be treated as persons, because of what they have been and the relationships and behaviour previously shown. The insane and mentally disturbed may be treated as persons because of past or future behaviour, but these definitions smack of special pleading. We do not really need fancy arguments, or philosophical dogmas to recognize in these cases that we are in the presence of shadows of humanity. They are so like people, yet not fully responsive. Such shadow-life makes us more gentle and careful to guard their rights and dignity. We do not debate their person-hood. We respond to humanity in its need.

M. FINANCE

Euthanasia is also a matter of money. In a society where there are more older people requiring more care, economics is a vital factor. For many old people facing increasing inflation and diminishing income, the question of economic survival often becomes a question of life itself. Poverty is still a problem for old people (as for many others). Pride makes it difficult to accept even the paid-for 'charity' of government. The costs, too, of caring for and treating physically and mentally handicapped children, the insane, the elderly and the incurably ill are high, and put further strain on health and social services budgets. Can we afford to keep people alive? Is this how money ought to be spent?

Many of us feel profoundly uneasy that matters of life and death have a financial aspect. It would be foolish to deny this part of the problem. It is equally foolish to pretend that the heart of the pro- or anti-euthanasia case really rests on questions of economics. There are other moral and religious values at stake (V).

N. MEDICAL TECHNIQUES AND THEIR LIMITS

No one would deny the progress of medicine. We all benefit from such progress, whether we like it or not. People are uneasy, however, whether medicine has become 'too big for its boots'. The ability to transplant major organs, implant babies in infertile wombs and to resuscitate the apparently dead make us a trifle uneasy. Where will it all end? We have the feeling that some expressions of medicine are unnatural. Yet this notion is fraught with problems. What is natural today was certainly not natural a century ago. Today's miracle is tomorrow's commonplace in medicine. What is extraordinary today may be extremely ordinary in the near future. How then are limits of medicine to be approached?

Some seek to draw a distinction between 'ordinary' and 'extraordinary' forms of treatment. This distinction is obviously fluid, but the 'ordinary' will include all the normal forms of treatment, whereas the 'extraordinary' will be untried and untested, unusual, dangerous or expensive drugs or techniques. The 'ordinary' means would be available and used without question. The 'extraordinary' would be used, if the doctor thought it appropriate or if there were some overwhelming need on the part of the patient or relatives for such measures to be attempted.

This still leaves the need for criteria by which to judge and safeguard against the misapplication of meddlesome medicine. The rough standard is that treatment should offer some reasonable chance of an appreciable duration of desirable life at an acceptable cost of suffering. The quality matters as much as the quantity. This still leaves definitional and practical problems with 'reasonable chance', 'appreciable duration', 'desirable' and 'acceptable'. Here the doctors must decide in concert with the patient and relatives.

When the limits of medicine are at their starkest is when a patient is facing death. Death spells defeat. How often we hear doctors say, 'There was nothing more we could do'. This ought not to be some great confession of failure, for they may have done too much. That we are unable to keep human life going at all costs is part of what it means to be human. However, to accept the fact and reality of death as a limit is not the same as actively to seek that death. Patients do wish to be safeguarded from the excesses of modern medicine. They neither want to die twice by continual resuscitations nor to be guinea pigs for drastic techniques or drugs with little hope of improvement in life. Euthanasia is not the only answer, for proper legal and professional control will serve!

O. LEGISLATION
We have seen the necessity for careful legislation to safeguard both doctors and patients in cases of transplants and neo-natal care of the severely handicapped. But in examining the area of euthanasia it is clear that the desire of some is for legal permission

to claim euthanasia as a right. In 1936, 1950 and 1969 the Voluntary Euthanasia Society sought to introduce bills in both Houses for voluntary euthanasia. In recent times more attention has focused on the famous debate over the EXIT publication, giving details of how to commit suicide successfully. The heart of the pro-euthanasia legal case rests on the notions of compassion for all who suffer, the free will of people to decide their own fate, and the basic human right of an individual to do whatever he or she likes with their own body. Such attempts at legislation face a number of problems.

The first is to ensure the valid consent of the patient. In a situation of pain and distress, in an unfamiliar setting of hospital, or at home under pressure both from the presence or absence of relatives, how would it be possible to safeguard the patient's genuine desire from unwarranted pressure? Problems likewise would arise over insurance policies and inheritance questions. If someone chooses to die, are they entitled to the benefits of their insurance policies? If relatives are to benefit from such a death, how can it be ensured that there has been no untoward force on the patient. It has been suggested that people might sign a form earlier in life which comes into effect only in circumstances of incurable disease or handicapping accident. The problem then is whether we are to be bound by decisions made many years previously and to what extent our attitudes and beliefs may change. Life may seem the more precious, the less we have left. The academic possibility of euthanasia is remote from the emotionally charged setting of the actual possibility. Such emotional pressures again make psychiatric assessment of the patient's rationality and responsibility difficult. Some fear that any move to legalize euthanasia would have unpleasant consequences. The relatives will have guilt added to their grief. Did we pressurize too much? Did my loss of temper and cruel words force the decision? There might also be concern as to the effect on the doctor–patient relationship. If the doctor has a piece of paper and power to assist death, then patients, especially the elderly and confused, may be hesitant as to the doctor's action and therefore, be unwilling to follow instructions. The greatest fear, however, is of the possible extension of voluntary euthanasia to the area of compulsory euthanasia. This is yet another example of the wedge argument. If you allow voluntary euthanasia now, it opens the door to compulsory euthanasia in practice on infants, the abnormal and the unacceptable, racially, morally and intellectually. Spectres of genocide and the policies of 'superior races' are conjured up in the debate. Care needs to be exercised in evaluating such 'consequences', for they are speculative and not necessarily the only or the most profitable ones.

In addition to these problems over legislation for euthanasia, there remains the question of effective safeguards. Who is to ensure that the law is observed and how will that be done? As with capital punishment, mistakes are fatal and cannot be undone. Many people feel that the number of legislative problems is so great that there can be no real possibility of legalized euthanasia.

P. VALUE AND DEFINITION OF A PERSON (see L above)

Q. WHO DECIDES?
The basic claim of the Voluntary Euthanasia Society is that we all have a right to die. If there is to be any decision taken to die, then the individual should be free to choose death. Some respond that any decision to harm oneself shows a disturbed mind, and so rules out that person making any decision. These are two different situations which are crucial. The first is where the person is in full possession of faculties and able to decide properly, the other, where the person is unable to make such a decision.

If the person is able to decide, then is the choice to be left to him or her? The first issue is that of 'ability to decide'. What constitutes such ability? A normal, rational person may be the standard we apply. But then do normal, rational people wish to end their lives? The criticism of any such decision to end life (as with suicide) is that in itself it constitutes the sign of an unbalanced mind. If you want to do harm to yourself, there must be something wrong with you. The difficulty is that view seems unable to appreciate the desperate condition that some people reach in illness or suffering, so desperate, in fact, that death seems like a 'happy release'. Even if we allow the serious plea of someone to end life, that still leaves the question of how to judge such a plea. We do not allow people to do whatever they like with their own bodies. Hence the laws which seek to protect individuals even against themselves. Death is a final harm to oneself, even if that 'harm' seems a good escape. Thus inevitably others—family, doctors and advisers—are involved both in judging the appeal to end life and in seeking to help the patient who makes the plea.

The other situation is where the patient is unable to plead for his death. He may be unconscious, senile or mentally disturbed to such an extent that there is little or no possibility of such an appeal being made. If there was a previous rational time, when a decision that life was to be ended under these circumstances was taken, it still leaves the question of how binding that decision is under the new circumstances (see O). But often there is no such decision to which to refer and thus the doctors, family and society must pass a judgement. We have already seen how any decision by the family may add to a burden of guilt then and later. If the doctor is to decide, then there are questions of the role of the medical practitioner, and the interpretation and trust by others of the medical profession and its role, and the problem of who is to control and check the doctor's decisions. We have recent cases where doctors have appealed to local authorities to take custody of a child requiring treatment, which parents wished to deny. The law and its representatives have therefore a final say and act as a safeguard. Thus doctors may be brought to trial at present for assisting the ending of life both of the elderly and of the young by active treatment, which is designed to hasten death. By such legal action, society is refusing to allow the doctor to act willy-nilly. The doctor is responsible both to the professional bodies and to the law of the land.

R. CONSEQUENCES

In talking of euthanasia, consequences are important. For the patient, they are fatal. For the family, they are seen as a release or as long-term guilt. They would certainly change the role of doctors and nurses as popularly seen today. However, there is a form of argument in the debate which is important. This is the 'wedge' argument. It states that, if we permit euthanasia, even under limited circumstances, then we shall end up with death control for many other people. The fear is that giving an inch on the value of life will lead to the taking of a mile. Not only the willing would die, but also the unwilling, whom the ruling group found unacceptable. Today the senile and malformed; tomorrow the five-foot-seven inches, bespectacled Scotsman (that is, the author). Such a line of argument depends on knowing likely consequences. This is its weakness, for there may be another set of equally plausible consequences, which are more favourable. More money will be left for the care of others. People will be relieved from suffering and watching others suffer. The uncertainty of consequences should make us cautious about basing a moral decision on consequences alone.

S. PUBLIC OPINION

In the case of suicide, public opinion has moved from regarding it as a crime to seeing it as a cry for help or sign of illness. The attitude towards euthanasia is more confused. No one wants to suffer or to make others suffer unnecessarily. However, people are very concerned about life and that every attempt to sustain life is made. Part of this may well be the fear of death. Mixed up with this is fear of pain and increasing expectations of pain control by the medical world. People do not expect to have to suffer, nor see their relatives suffer. In that sense, the hospice movement and increasingly improving geriatric care have made the necessity for euthanasia laws seem more remote. There are, of course, many who affirm the right to die, but most people seem still to cling to life and to be gravely concerned when situations arise, where assisted death is involved. It is not simply legal unease, but deeply held public concern and reaction are involved. What is not so clear is the extent to which the public will match their concern to maintain life by their acceptance of financial responsibilities.

T. ALTERNATIVES

In counselling those contemplating euthanasia for themselves or their relatives young or old, alternatives must be genuine ones. There is little comfort from the hope that round the corner some medical discovery will transform the situation. Yet even that hope and possibility are enough to sustain some, particularly those responsible for young children, who are severely handicapped.

For some, the alternative of life itself—no matter the quality or kind of life—is sufficient. To be alive and to be able to experience anything at all is enough reason to preserve life. This still leaves problems for those who have no 'experience' and yet are technically alive. However, in the cases of the elderly, mentally disturbed and severely handicapped, any alternative to euthanasia will mean a high degree of care and the consequent requirements of time, staff expertise and finance. If we value life highly, it will be costly in many respects.

The crux of the problem of alternatives is how the individual affected perceives the alternatives. Where the life ahead seems to offer nothing but pain and loneliness, or decreasing abilities and increasing handicap and limitation, it is little wonder that some desire an 'easy death'. A genuine alternative must mean relative freedom from pain, real care and affection from others, and help to cope with the frustrations and limitations ageing or illness will bring. It is the absence of these alternatives which may seem the basis of a plea for euthanasia.

Whether it is in coping with alternatives or the choice between alternatives, individual and family counselling will play a part. This is extremely difficult, however, with the elderly and the mentally disturbed. In these cases, it is unlikely there will be a present request for euthanasia and any previous request will be subject to the problems mentioned earlier (O). Such vulnerable people demand even greater caution and care than those in situations where rational choices are made with full awareness of the consequences.

U. FEARS AND EMOTIONS

Illness and contemplation of death are deeply emotional issues. It is hard for any of us to be neutral or objective in these matters. Our human limitations are all too real. The long history of funeral rites and bereavement practices bears witness to the fears and emotions concerning death and dying. Many do fear death, for death is for them final, absolute and unknown. Even for those who are confident that death is not the end, there is apprehension and fear both at departing from life and at entering into an unknown experience. Recent opinion suggests that, despite the reality of such fears, it is not death that frightens people. It is the pain involved in dying. For many the issue of euthanasia is about freedom from pain. It is either the patient's freedom from pain on his or her demand, or the helpful compassion from family and medical staff, to ease that pain. As we have seen above (T), if real freedom from pain is an alternative to the pain of dying, euthanasia may not seem necessary as an escape. Part of the problem is that the patient may be afraid of a 'meddlesome medicine', which strives officiously to bring people back from the edge of death, only to die twice; this is a real fear.

The emotional tangle of patient, family, medical nursing staff, and of friends makes clear judgement difficult. Guilt, compassion, apprehension concerning the future are all part of the emotions involved. These fears and emotions need to be recognized, and the people concerned need to come to terms with them. Is the desire for or resistance to euthanasia merely an emotional response? Are there genuine reasons behind the reaction? Are these sufficient grounds for action?

V. MORAL AND RELIGIOUS VALUES (see F, I, P)

We shall discuss the Christian moral principles involved below, but it is clear that many different moral principles are at work in the euthanasia debate. It is important to draw a distinction in the debate between two different kinds of arguments. The first kind are arguments based on principles. The second kind are arguments based on consequences. These are often confused. There is a world of difference between doing something because it is right in itself, regardless of any consequences, and doing something because in the end it will lead to better consequences. In the latter case I may do something evil in order to achieve good. In the former case I would never do anything evil, regardless of the good consequences that *might* accrue.

In dealing with the issue of euthanasia, we must separate clearly principles from consequences. The kinds of principles at work are: (i) Those concerning life and death. Is life to be valued at all costs? Is there an important distinction between quantity and quality of life? Is death the end? Is such an end to be feared? Our moral attitudes to life and death are important, as is the religious value, if any, that we place on them; (ii) Choice and freedom are important. Is such an individual choice sovereign? Are we free to choose to do anything to ourselves? Should my choices involve the criminal or morally debatable action of others? (iii) The issue of rights is part of the moral debate. Have I the right to die? Have I the duty to assist others to die? Has society any rights at stake here? How are we to weigh up respective rights and their order of priority? (iv) Pain and suffering and our moral attitude to them affects our view of euthanasia. Is pain always bad and to be avoided at all costs? Has suffering a positive role to play in life? Does suffering necessarily destroy? (v) Happiness is involved morally. What makes people happy and how is this defined and measured? Have we the right to happiness? Have others the duty to make us happy? Is happiness to be pursued at all costs? (vi) We must consider compassion. Can love permit pain and suffering? Does love mean doing whatever another wishes? Does compassion relieve every situation? Is compassion more about my feeling good than the patient being relieved?

These six areas (and many more) are the kinds of moral and religious values at stake in the debate as well as the social, professional and legal issues. These must be clarified and the various views of those directly involved and affected stated. Any decision which ignores these moral questions is difficult to defend and to propound as a legitimate basis for action.

W. COMPASSION

For some the issue of rights is the heart of the pro-euthanasia case. For others it is the issue of compassion. They are confronted by the genuine fear and pain of the elderly, the mentally disturbed, the terminally ill, and the severely handicapped. Such suffering compels them to act in love to put an end to such suffering. No one can question the motive, though it is debated whether euthanasia is the only (or even a suitable) alternative for the compassionate person. There is little doubt that suffering should incite us to act. The issue is what form such actions should take.

Some suggest that compassion reveals more about our difficulty in seeing others in pain than the actual pain that others experience. Thus action to remove pain all together, for example, by euthanasia, would be really to relieve ourselves rather than the sufferer. Of course, feelings of compassion are often genuine, but mere feeling is not sufficient to make a difference to the patient. Thus for any action taken on the basis of compassion, we need to ensure, as far as is possible, that it will help the situation.

Some are hesitant as to the right of others to interfere even on the grounds of compassion. This is especially the case where it may involve final and irreversible action. Genuine compassion seeks to help the other, and that means defining and knowing what will actually help. The compassionate person is looking for alternatives to the present pain and situation (see T). These can only be pursued if the motives, rights, and consequences are fully weighed.

X. WORLD-WIDE CONTEXT

There are those who argue for euthanasia on the grounds of global problems. An ever-increasing world population, diminishing natural resources and an ageing population in many western nations have led some to posit a kind of 'survival of the fittest' or a willingness to step aside, in order to allow others an opportunity for better life. It is difficult to see what specific difference any legislation to permit euthanasia would make, for the number espousing such 'survival' views would be limited. Yet it is the fear that such legislation might open the door to such philosophies, which lies behind the wedge/consequentialist argument. There seems, however, in logic no more reason for fastening on death and euthanasia rather than abortion and the beginnings of life as a more successful way of dealing with the global problems. That said, it remains true that we must all act to take account of the global problems, though this need not have anything to do with euthanasia.

Y. DEFORMITY AND HANDICAP

In the strict sense of 'euthanasia', the issue of taking the life of a severely deformed person is possible. Within the common understanding of a request by the patient to die, this is unusual in the cases of handicap and deformity, which are most hotly debated. That is those affecting neonates and young children.

Technically this comes under the heading of infanticide. As the young child is unable to choose, parents or medical staff are forced to make a choice. Apart from the obvious emotional, moral and legal issues in such a choice, there are the incalculable problems of knowing exactly how severe the deformity will be in the long term, how much improvement is actually possible, and how new medical advances might affect both the previous categories. So often the handicap seems more a problem for the onlooker, than for the handicapped person. We must say 'seems', for it is hard to know exactly what the severely deformed think and feel, and what their own desire for life and fulfilment can be. It is the exceptional cases, where a poet emerges or a literary genius is discovered by some teaching or technical accident, which makes us cautious with the usual and often painful 'normality' of others. Who knows what abilities might be there, waiting to be properly tapped and which, if discovered, might transform the lives of all those involved.

We have seen below that one working criterion for decisions of life and death in practice is 'reasonable expectation of adequate quality of life'. The problem is that the definitions of 'reasonable', 'expectation', 'adequate', and 'quality' tend to be reached by 'normal' people with reference to 'normal' life. Is it just to use such criteria for the deformed and handicapped? On the other hand, if not these criteria, what basis for judgement is there?

In considering all the factors, we are brought to see the way moral and religious principles underlie and affect the way we use facts in discussion and the interpretation and significance attached to them. We now consider how the Christian contemplates the first important principles.

2 First important principles

What are the principles which the Christian uses when he comes to the issue of euthanasia? In light of these principles, what order of priorities will operate in the decision-making?

(1) HAS SCRIPTURE SOME PARTICULAR TEACHING OR PRINCIPLES WHICH ARE RELEVANT HERE?

(i) Creation

Are there particular principles to be derived from these sources?

1. *Natural Law:* In one sense, life and death are the most natural things in the world. We are born and we die. Yet we are not happy about dying. We not only fear death, but we are endowed with a strong will to live. We seek to preserve our own lives. That is a natural feature of men and women. They want to live. Thus death is seen as an enemy to be resisted. Yet death is part of the natural processes of the world. Our emotional response to death hints that we regard life as more important than death and the preservation of life as an important human activity.

The euthanasia debate is bedevilled with appeals to natural and unnatural means of sustaining and ending life. Modern medicine and technology have ensured that 'what is natural' is constantly changing in content. Almost all medicine is an interference with nature. Thus any appeal to 'let nature take its course' is to make a key value judgement about which situations we wish to accept and which to resist. What is clear in general terms is that we do seek to preserve life and to resist death, unless there are overwhelming reasons to the contrary. The moral dilemma is which reasons constitute a sufficient basis for assisting or allowing death to occur.

2. *Man in the image of God:* From Gen. 1.27; 2.7, it is clear that man's relationship with God is important and different from the rest of creation.

> So God created man in his own image, in the image of God he created him; male and female he created them. (Gen. 1.27. NIV)

> And the Lord God formed man from the dust of the ground and breathed into his nostrils the breath of life, and man became a living being (Gen. 2.7, NIV).

God is seen as the Creator, Author, Sustainer, Preserver and Lord of life. All life, whether human or not, stems from God. It is because life is God's that death is equally seen as depending on God. God created man. To be a creature is to be at the call and disposal of the Creator. This is exactly man's situation. Life and death are not in the hands of man, but rest in the hands of God. He is the Sovereign One, and that sovereignty must include ultimate control over life and death. He gives life and he takes it away. The Bible clearly emphasizes that life is the gift of God. It is the very breath of God. To attempt to control that life without reference to God, and to imagine that it is man's own to do with what he pleases, is to rebel against God and to seek to usurp his place and role.

The notion of life as a gift from God brings certain responsibilities. When man is given life, it is in the form of a loan. Our lives do not belong to us. We cannot do whatever we like with our lives. The created man is a steward of God. He is answerable to God for the whole of creation and for the way in which he uses and cares for that created order. This must also mean that we are stewards of God with respect to our lives. We are answerable and accountable to God for life itself and how we use that life. We are not free to return the loan whenever we feel like it.

The importance of the image of God is not purely in our attitude to our own lives, but it also affects other people.

> Whoever sheds the blood of man
> by man shall his blood be shed;
> for in the image of God
> has God made man (Gen. 9.6, NIV).

As made in the image of God, man is given a worth and dignity. Thus a person's worth is not a matter of self-assessment nor of social significance nor contribution. It is a result of being created in the image of God. Thus the dignity of man makes human life important and to be treated with reverence. Part of this dignity is exemplified in the exercising of dominion in creation. In modern terms, this means that man is answerable to God for his creation and the use of science, technology and medicine. As good stewards, we are to use these things in ways which reinforce and preserve man's God-given dignity. But as stewards, we are accountable to God for that usage.

3. *Conscience:* Obviously our conscience is closely bound up with our will to live and to preserve life. Our picture of the murderer is of a person tortured by guilt and suffering from a bad conscience. In fact, many people's consciences seem very weak and to have little effect on their lives. Yet a major unease in the area of euthanasia is that of how people will live with consequences of assisting in death. Knowing that they were involved in a decision to aid death, or even in the act of death itself, may be too much to bear. Some would suggest that no matter how strong or weak a person's conscience might be, that conscience is considered relevant at all suggests that there is a crucial point concerning life and its sacredness. The possibility of a guilty conscience indicates that such taking of life is wrong.

Others counter by suggesting that it is harder to live with one's conscience if one has permitted more pain and suffering and failed to act to deliver people from dignity and suffering. The sin of omission is as serious as the sin of commission.

Both these views of the role of conscience depend on the principles which operate in and through conscience, and these in turn may reflect the training and education of conscience as well as any natural, intuitive basis.

4. *Creation Ordinances:* (see para. 2 above)

5. *The Fall:* The picture of the Fall is one of disruption and dislocation. By man's sinfulness and disobedience, the righteous God passed this judgement,

> Cursed is the ground because of you;
> through painful toil you will eat of it
> all the days of your life.
> It will produce thorns and thistles for you,
> and you will eat the plants of the field.
> By the sweat of your brow
> you will eat your food
> until you return to the ground,
> since from it you were taken;
> for dust you are
> and to dust you will return (Gen. 3.17–19, NIV).

Death and suffering are often interpreted as a direct result of the Fall. Death is accordingly an aberration in the world. The further proof of this, it is argued, is the first murder by Cain of Abel. Man's life comes to an end at the hands of his brother man. Thus we have in the Old Testament the development of laws concerning the regulation of life and death.

There are, however, misunderstandings which can arise here. Life is never seen as the be-all and end-all of man. The life we have is creaturely life: it is temporal. Life has an end. There is no absolute greatness or supreme value in life. Life has no intrinsic worth. Life has only meaning, worth, and even definition with reference to God. Thus it is as wrong to desire to live at all costs trying to cling to this world and our existence in it, as to imagine that it is right to choose the manner and time of our own death.

Even with the garden picture, there is strong emphasis that fellowship with God continues, despite the Fall and the curse. This continuity of fellowship develops in the New Testament to seeing death not as a terminus, but as a transition.

(ii) The Old Testament

What particular principles may be derived from these sources?

1. *Covenant and Law:* Within the Decalogue, there are strict rules governing matters of life and death. The fifth commandment is, 'Thou shalt not kill' (Exod. 20.13). For some this is the last and only word necessary in relation to euthanasia. This is difficult to sustain for the implication here is of murder, and it may be hotly disputed as to whether the motives of compassion involved in cases of euthanasia can in any sense be compared with those of a murderer. Yet it is still clear that the commandment does take seriously the sanctity of life and this must mean that our attitude to the taking of life ought to be extremely cautious.

2. *Wisdom Literature:* The difficult book of Job contains two kinds of themes relevant to the euthanasia debate. When Job is encouraged to take his own life and escape from the horrors of his experience, he refuses, arguing that we must accept trouble from the hands of God as well as good. In sharp contrast, stand the description of the pointlessness and pain of life.

> Why is light given to those in misery,
> and life to the bitter of soul,
> to those who long for death that does not come,
> who search for it more than for hidden treasure,
> who are filled with gladness
> and rejoice when they reach the grave? (Job 3.20-2, NIV).

And again,

> Or a man may be chastened on a bed of pain
> with constant distress in his bones,
> so that his very being finds food repulsive
> and his soul loathes the choicest meal.
> His flesh wastes away to nothing,
> and his bones, once hidden, now stick out.
> His soul draws near to the pit,
> and his life to the messengers of death (Job 33.19-22, NIV).

The conflict in Job's own mind between a belief in the sovereignty of God in all matters of life and death and his bitter personal experience is the very stuff of the book.

The Psalmist, like the writers of the creation accounts, gives man a high place of dignity.

> You made him a little lower than the heavenly beings
> and crowned him with glory and honour (Ps. 8.5, NIV).

Psalms 22 to 28 give a clear picture of a man coping with the very depths of depression, oppression and fear. All share the hope of an optimistic outcome, if the believer but continues to trust in God. Yet the limited span of man's life is clearly presented:

> The length of our days is seventy years—
> or eighty, if we have the strength;
> yet their span is but trouble and sorrow,
> for they quickly pass, and we fly away (Ps. 90.10, NIV).

Death here is seen as inevitable, yet there is no thought of escaping from life or its troubles. Death will come all too soon, it seems, even in a troubled life.

3. *The Prophets:* There is no substantive discussion of the issues

of euthanasia in the prophetic material, though some would argue that the stories of the fiery furnace and the lion's den show that God preserved human life in spite of the worst that men can do. It might also be argued that the patient enduring of suffering leads to life and vindication. Obviously, however, the context of these events is very far from that of euthanasia.

(iii) The New Testament

What principles may be derived from these sources?

1. *Redemption:* The New Testament pictures of redemption include the notion of victory over death. Death is seen as an enemy to be defeated. Christ overcomes the enemy by his death and resurrection. Yet within the gospels themselves there are pointers to that overcoming of death. In the midst of the miracle stories, there are two accounts of raising people from the dead. The son of the widow of Nain and Lazarus are called back to life. Some would add the raising of Jairus' daughter as a third. John's Gospel makes the theological point most clearly by framing the incident with Christ's words:

> I am the resurrection and the life. He who believes in me will live, even though he dies: and whoever lives and believes in me will never die (John 11.25–26, NIV).

Christ then goes on to summon Lazarus from the tomb. It is clear that an essential part of redemption is Christ's control over death. Christ is the one who intervenes in situations of sickness and death to restore and renew life. This must be linked with Christ's own suffering. Not only is Christ concerned to relieve the suffering of others and does so; but he is willing himself to suffer and die to achieve redemption and victory over death. Jesus showed where suffering and, even the final apparently meaningless event of death, can lead: to life for all, to redemption and to a new creation.

The idea that there is a purpose in life, even in suffering, may also be derived from the accounts of Simeon and Anna in Luke 4. The picture is of two old people who live only in the hope that the Messiah will come. When Christ as a child is brought to the

Temple, both prophesy about Christ's role in redemption. Simeon's words are still used in worship in the Nunc Dimittis.

> Sovereign Lord, as you have promised,
> you now dismiss your servant in peace.
> For my eyes have seen your salvation,
> which you have prepared in the sight of all people,
> a light for revelation to the Gentiles
> and for glory to your people Israel (Luke 4.29–32, NIV).

The purpose for living completed, Simeon feels ready to die. This theme of life and death resting in God's hands, rather than man's own, is also obvious in the parable of the rich man, who pulls down his barns to build bigger ones planning for a life of pleasure and ease.

> But God said to him, 'You fool! This very night your life will be demanded from you. Then who will get what you have prepared for yourself?' (Luke 12.20, NIV).

The main point is the nature of true riches, but that point is made *assuming* God's control over life and death.

2. Kingdom ethics: Within the life, example and teaching of Jesus, it is obvious that compassion for the suffering is a cornerstone. Those who bear the name of Christ are to follow this example of love and compassion. The problem is that we do not always know what is the truly compassionate action. Obviously, the alleviation of pain is crucial, but if that is only achieved by the taking of life, how are we to act? There is no specific ethical guide for this in the New Testament pages. Compassion is proclaimed, along with an emphasis on the importance of eternal life. In Christ, death is not the end, but leads to a fuller and deeper quality of life in relation to God. Resurrection is the key to this possibility, for Paul argues that if Christ did not rise from the dead, Christian preaching and faith are useless, Christians are liars, still in their sins, and those who have died in Christ are lost. Paul concludes,

> If only for this life we have hope in Christ, we are to be pitied more than all men (1 Cor. 15.19, NIV).

Death is an enemy. But it is a defeated enemy, whose power holds no terror for the Christian. From this, it is possible to argue both that death is to be resisted, yet is not ultimately to be feared. Christians thus would seek to resist death, but not at all costs.

3. *Paul's ethics:* It is clear that in Paul's life there were many occasions when he faced both suffering and death. Paul felt the pull of death, not for its own sake, but as a gateway to life beyond; yet he resisted the attraction.

> I am torn between the two: I desire to depart and be with Christ, which is better by far; but it is more necessary for you that I remain in the body (Phil. 1.23-4, NIV).

Likewise at Philippi itself. Paul and Silas restrain the jailer from taking his own life, when he thinks he has failed in his duty to keep the prisoners in custody. They do not, however, offer a theological or philosophical argument against taking his life. The appeal is purely pragmatic and common-sense. No prisoner had escaped (Acts 16).

Paul, as we have seen in 1 Cor. 15, propounded a strong view of resurrection as the key to the defeat of death. Yet his emphasis is not only on the importance of a life beyond the grave, but also of that quality of eternal life as a present reality, affecting people's behaviour here and now (for example, 1 Thess. 5.10).

In some ways Paul seems to see this life as a process to be completed before we enter the fullness of eternal life. In this way, suffering may have a positive role to play in the shaping of the Christian. He writes:

> . . . but we also rejoice in our sufferings, because we know that suffering produces perseverance; perseverance, character; and character, hope (Rom. 5.3-4, NIV).

In a real sense, Paul is saying that suffering can be good for people. This is in keeping with his strong sense of the sovereignty of God, for a few chapters later he writes:

> And we know that in all things God works for the good of those who love him, who have been called according to his purpose (Rom. 8.28, NIV).

Following from this, it seems that the active seeking of any final and total escape from suffering in death is not open to the Christian. His times are in the hands of God, and there may be lessons to be gained from the processes of suffering.

4. *The Pastoral Epistles:* This same theme and approach marks the writings in 1 Peter. The letter is written to those in the midst of suffering and persecution (1 Pet. 1.17). For the writer any suffering which comes because of being a Christian is neither surprising nor an excuse for being down-hearted. Rather it is a joy and privilege to participate in the sufferings of Christ. The key passage concludes:

> So then, those who suffer according to God's will should commit themselves to their faithful Creator and continue to do good (1 Pet. 4.19, NIV).

This does not imply that all suffering is good, but that there is a suffering which necessarily comes to the Christian as a Christian and that this is not to be rejected, but accepted. It is doubtful whether such suffering is similar to the pain which may lead to the desire to die, though there are extreme cases of the torture of Christians, which are relevant here.

For the pastoral writers, the present trials of life were of little significance in comparison with the glories of the life to come. Yet that can be no ground for an escape from the present reality.

(2) HAS TRADITION SOME PARTICULAR TEACHING OR PRINCIPLES WHICH ARE RELEVANT HERE?

Traditionally life has been seen as a gift from God. Therefore it was not proper for man to seek to end his own life. The long history of the prohibition of suicide and the horrific treatment meted out to the body and the relatives of the suicide show the force of the traditional rejection of taking one's own life. The idea that God controlled man's life and his death meant that there could be no attempt to take life merely for the sake of escaping suffering. Some might argue that the principle of double effect makes euthanasia a possibility if the primary motive is the alleviation of another's pain. In practice, many doctors do give fatal doses of pain-killers at the point where there is no other way of overcoming the patient's distress. This, it is claimed, is not to take life, but to provide comfort and release from pain. The double-effect is that death ensues.

In dealing with a tradition which must regard euthanasia with deep suspicion as a taking of divine prerogatives into human hands, it would require some strong ground to overthrow the weight of that tradition.

(3) HAS THE SPIRIT OR THE CHURCH SOME PARTICULAR TEACHING OR PRINCIPLES WHICH ARE RELEVANT HERE?

Among church people there is a genuine division of opinion and both wings would claim the support of the Holy Spirit. The one wing bases its case on the central Christian virtue of love and compassion. Such love cannot accept nor allow that people should suffer unnecessarily. It destroys the dignity of people. Euthanasia is seen as a potential virtue, for it allows some ministry of love to the suffering and dying. Obviously, no one is arguing for a free-for-all nor for euthanasia simply on demand. Yet there is a deep concern for Christians to take a positive stand in this ministry of compassion and release.

In contrast, there are other Christians who are concerned about any form of euthanasia both in terms of principles and consequences. The likely consequences and legal problems are so great as to make the whole exercise improbable. Nevertheless, it is the principle of life and God's ultimate control of life which is to be preserved. We have no right to take the lives of others, nor to assist them in the taking of their own lives. Rather the truly Christian task is to minister to those who are suffering in both a physical and spiritual way, believing that it is possible to find sufficient resources in Christ to cope and to overcome.

It is hard to see how we can decide between such views on the basis of the Spirit and the Church alone. Yet we must do justice to both wings in approaching the issue in all its complexity.

As with the abortion issue, we are left with the problems of how we apply these principles to the actual cases we are facing. Admitting the genuine problem there, it is still clear that we do need principles and that, if they are important to us, we must struggle to apply them realistically.

There are two main principles at stake. These are the principles of compassion and the sanctity of life. Obviously, both principles are important and there are ways of expressing them together. Nevertheless, there does come a point with a patient where a decision to continue treatment, to remove treatment, or to take active termination must be faced. It is then that one principle is seen to be primary.

3 Aims, goals and objectives

Given clarification of the basic principles and some order of priorities, we must clarify our objectives in the situation we are facing. Again, if we assume a counselling situation, we need to be clear concerning our role, the desirable and the possible outcomes and actions, the motives and the consequences. If our aim is to help the patient, his or her relatives or the doctor come to a decision, we need to help them clarify their aims, goals and objectives both in this particular case and in general. We may not be happy with their choice of objectives and it would be important to explore why that was the case. Nevertheless, we might still feel obliged to help them understand their own goals, the best ways of achieving these goals and the likely and possible consequences. We would also seek to offer support and help in their coping with their own decision, whatever the outcome. Otherwise, our advice is really conditional on it being accepted. We are saying, 'I will support you only if you do what I want'. This is thus a directive form of advice and we are really making the decision for the other person.

4 Alternatives, possibilities and choices

In the case of euthanasia, the alternatives are stark. Death or a continued life of suffering are the options. At least this is often how it seems to the patient. One key alternative to the choice of death is the likely hope of alleviation of pain and suffering or some possible improvement in the quality of life to be lived. It is vital that such hope is genuine. Many feel that recent and continued advances in pain control do offer real grounds for hope and that this should be explored as fully as possible. Others point to the continued possibility of improvements in medical care and techniques again offering hope of improved life. For others, it is not merely the physical issues of suffering which are at stake, but more importantly, it is to help people psychologically and spiritually to cope with their suffering. This is fine, in theory, but it is extremely difficult with the senile, the insane and the severely abnormal. Yet it may still be possible to minister love and comfort in real ways to those whose grasp on reality seems very different from our own.

Many see the hospice movement as the real ground of alternatives for all of us, patient, doctor and relatives alike. The total context of care, the specific forms of pain-control, and the healthy attitudes to life and death seem to coalesce in the practice of many of the hospices.

5   Other people's viewpoints

Christians are very good at propounding their viewpoint, but perhaps less able to listen to the views of others and to do these views full justice. There are many people involved in and affected by the issues of euthanasia, and all too many viewpoints are expressed. These views must be presented, understood, weighed and then accepted or rejected. Behind the viewpoints, there are central issues of difference at stake. These must be clarified and distilled as the proper ground for decision-making. To arrive at this point all the opinions must be taken seriously.

6   Final reflections

When I teach Christian ethics, people become annoyed. They keep asking me what I think and believe. I have views and am only too happy to propound them as forcefully as I can. But in teaching, my aim is not so much to make disciples for my views as to clarify for others what is involved in their moral decision-making. It is not very likely that most of us will face the question of euthanasia every day. Yet it is vital that we know where we stand, why we stand there, and that, in itself, may move us to action or to contribute to the very real debates and problems which are everyday occurrences in hospitals, law-courts, and among those who face the issues of suffering, life and death.

Conclusion

The initial intention was to apply this approach to the further areas of sexuality, marriage and divorce, economics, war and violence. Time and space prevented this, for it soon becomes evident that moral problems are more complex than first appearances suggest. I do not believe that this means that we all have to become geniuses to make moral decisions. It does mean that we need to work hard at being consistent and careful in dealing with every aspect of the issue facing us. The applications offered here are meant both as examples of how the method may be put to work, and also as contributions to a Christian approach to the life and death matters of abortion and euthanasia. It is the method itself which is important. The application of the method properly lies in the hands of all those facing moral problems and particularly of those who have the privilege and difficult task of counselling, advising and directing those who face problems. In education and training, success comes when the learner takes the teacher's ideas and applies them for himself or herself adding a distinctive contribution. My hope is that all those who teach ethics, train people to help in moral guidance, and those who face moral dilemmas will be able to apply some of the ideas here for their benefit and to the glory of God.

Further Reading

Baelz, P., *Ethics and Belief*. Sheldon Press 1977.

Barclay, W., *Ethics in a Permissive Society*. Fontana 1971.

Curran, C., *New Perspectives in Moral Theology*. University of Notre Dame 1974.

Dominian, J., *Proposals for a New Sexual Ethic*. Darton, Longman & Todd 1977.

Dunstan, G., *The Artifice of Ethics*. SCM Press 1974.

Fletcher, J., *Situation Ethics*. SCM Press 1966.

Hebblethwaite, B., *The Adequacy of Ethics*. Marshall Morgan & Scott 1981.

Mitchell, B., *Morality: Religious and Secular*. Clarendon Press 1980.

Piper, O., *Christian Ethics*. Nelson 1970.

Ramsey, P., *Basic Christian Ethics*. University of Chicago Press 1980

Thielicke, H., *Theological Ethics*. A & C Black 1968.

Ward, K., *Ethics and Christianity*. Allen & Unwin 1970.

Wogaman, J. P., *A Christian Method of Moral Judgement*. SCM Press 1976.

Index

abortion 27, 86–132
abstraction 2, 4, 13
agape 56, 69, 70
ageing 137–8
A.G.O. 83, 130, 171–2
alienation 2, 4, 13
antinomianism 69
A.P.C. 83–4, 130–1
Aquinas, Thomas 60
Augustine 60
authority 45, 49, 59, 62

behaviourism 9, 37–8
Bentham, Henry 32–4
Bible 16, 44, 77, 83, 87, 123–7,
   161–9; *see also* Scripture
biological view of morals 37–41
Bultmann, Rudolf 44

C.A.F. 82, 87–122, 133–60
Calvin, John 60
casuistry 64–9, 73
Church 60–3, 77, 83, 87, 111,
   128–9, 170–1
compassion 16, 124, 129, 157–9,
   167, 171
conscience 24–5, 51–3, 123, 163

consequences vii, 68, 72, 83, 94,
   100–2, 108, 120–1
covenant 53–4, 58, 124–5, 164
creation, creation ordinances 50–2,
   55, 58, 122, 124, 161–4

death 133, 138–9
De Bono, Edward 77
decalogue 53, 64, 124, 164
deformity 139, 143, 153, 156,
   159–61, 172
depersonalization 3, 8, 13
descriptivism 12, 21–6, 36
divorce 15–16, 72
double effect 108, 134–5, 147,
   169–70
Dominian, Jack 74

egoism 22–3, 31–4
emotion 20–1, 90–1, 156
emotivism 22–3, 27–31
empiricism 27, 29
euthanasia 86, 133–72
existentialism 4–5, 14, 22–3, 34–7,
   44, 48, 68, 84

Fall 52–3, 58, 124, 126
feeling 20, 26, 72, 79, 114, 159

F.I.P. 82, 111, 122–9, 149, 160–71
Fletcher, Joseph 69
foetus 87, 94–103, 107, 113, 116–18
Freud, Sigmund 38–9
futurity 3, 13

genetic fallacy 39, 43

handicap 141–2, 144, 147, 150, 155–6, 158–9
hedonism 22–3, 31–4, 39
homosexuality 15, 74, 110
hospice 138, 146, 155, 172

image 51–3, 58, 123
imitation 56–8
individualism 4–5, 14
industrialization 7, 15
intention 5, 20, 34–7, 66, 68, 90, 108, 120
intuition 22–6, 52, 78, 163

Kant, Immanuel 35
kingdom ethics 55–6, 58, 127, 167–8

lateral thinking 77
law 53–4, 56–8, 104–6, 116, 124–5, 134, 146–7, 152–4, 164
legalism 54, 64–9, 70–1, 73, 77
liberation 6–7, 117–18
life *see* sanctity of life
love 15, 56–7, 70–3, 74–5
Luther, Martin 60

marriage 15–16, 107
Marxism 39–40
materialism 9, 96
methodological presumption 64, 75–7

Mill, John S. 32–4
modernity 1
murder 29, 39, 67, 115

natural, naturalism, natural law 21–4, 26, 37–8, 50–3, 59, 64, 66–7, 78, 95, 118–19, 122–3, 144, 150, 161, 163
nuclear issues 59, 67

objective 14, 29, 48, 51, 72, 79, 80, 108, 143, 156
O.P.V. 84, 108, 131

pain 134, 136, 140–1 147–8, 155, 157–8, 169, 171
pastoral epistles 57–8, 127, 169
Pauline ethics 56–8, 127, 168–9
person 87, 96–7, 99, 107–8, 111–12, 118, 134, 139, 140, 149–50, 162
personalism 64, 70, 74–5, 77
Plato 21
pluralism, pluralization 9–11, 13, 15–16
positivism 70
pragmatism 70
prescriptivism 12, 22–3, 35–7, 70, 81
privatization 5–6, 14
prophets 54–5, 58, 126, 165
psycho-analytic view of morals 37–41

rape 87–8, 91, 102, 106, 112, 128
reason 20–6, 36, 51, 59, 69, 76, 79, 80, 153
redemption 55, 58, 126, 166–7
reductionism 8–9, 13, 15, 37–41
relativism 11–13, 15–16, 22, 28–31, 39, 47, 62, 66, 70

responsibility 33, 51-2, 76, 89-90, 93, 96, 104, 108, 141-2, 149, 152, 162
revelation 64
rights 6-7, 14, 87-90, 102-4, 140-2, 158-9

sanctity of life 29, 67, 98-9, 101-2, 107, 111-12, 128-9, 144, 147, 155, 164, 171
scepticism 18
science 8, 13, 15, 37, 41
Scripture 15-16, 44-58, 59-63, 67, 83, 111, 122-7, 129; *see also* Bible
secularization 7-8, 13-15, 43
sex 29, 59, 74, 87, 107, 111-14, 117, 122, 130
situation ethics 64, 69-73, 75, 77, 79
sociological view of morals 37-41

spirit 60-3, 64, 77, 83, 128-9, 170-1
subjective, subjectivism 14, 16, 29, 48, 61, 63, 75-9, 148
suicide 133, 135-6, 152-3, 155, 169

tolerance 12, 13, 15, 28-30
tradition 15, 36, 49, 50, 58-60, 62-4, 71, 77-8, 83, 127-9, 161-9
truth-telling 29, 39

urbanization 7, 15
utilitarianism 22-3, 32-4, 68, 72, 120, 141

will 20-1, 34-7
wisdom literature 54, 58, 125, 164-5
Wogaman, Philip 64